BEEN THERE
MYTHBUS

Challenging Success, Leadership, Business, and
What It Means Live Life To The Fullest

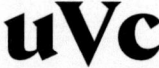 

Dear Andrew,

Stay excellent
keep learning
keep improving

Thank you for your dedication
and contributions to the continuing
success of MDB

blessings
Daniel
6/2024

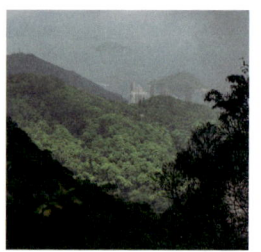

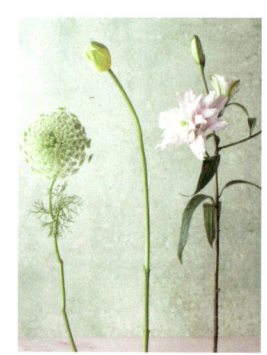

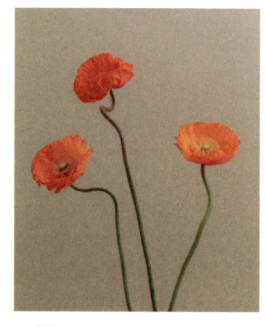

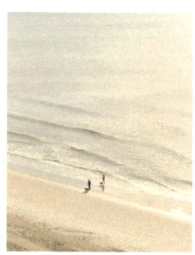

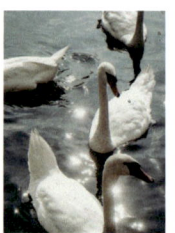

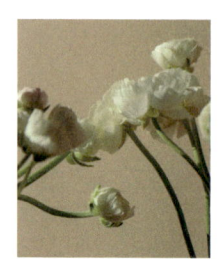

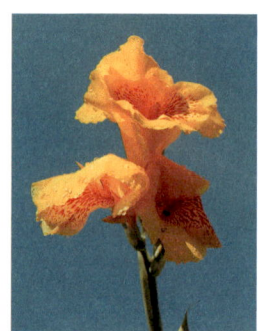

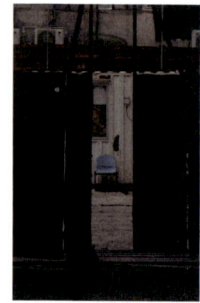

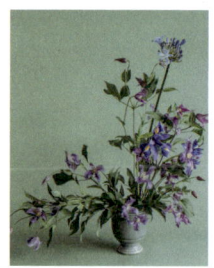

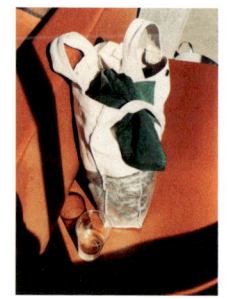

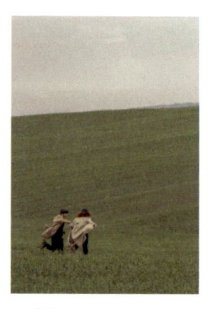

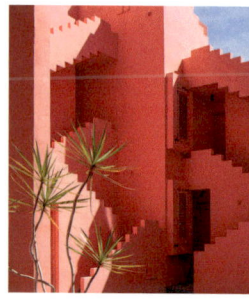

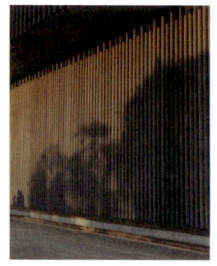

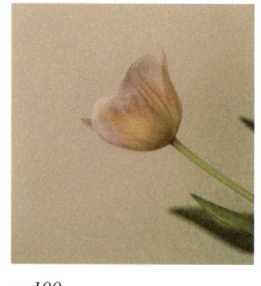

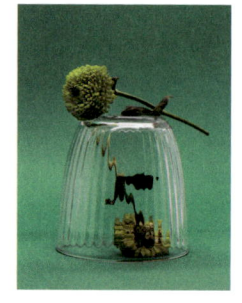

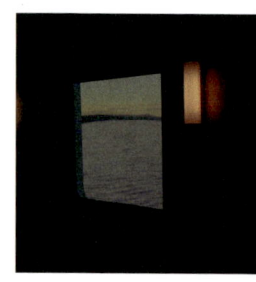

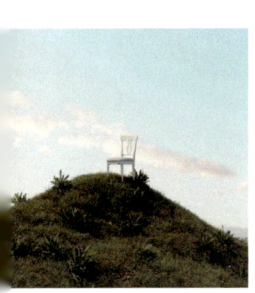

p. 118

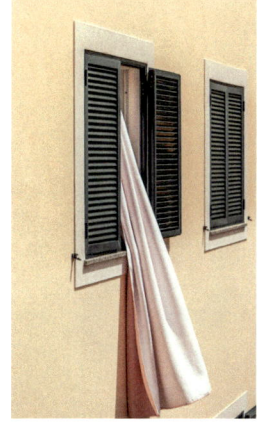

p. 124

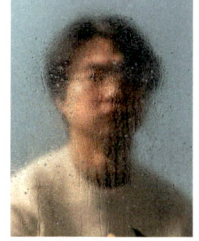

p. 130

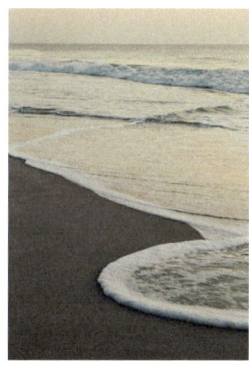

p. 136

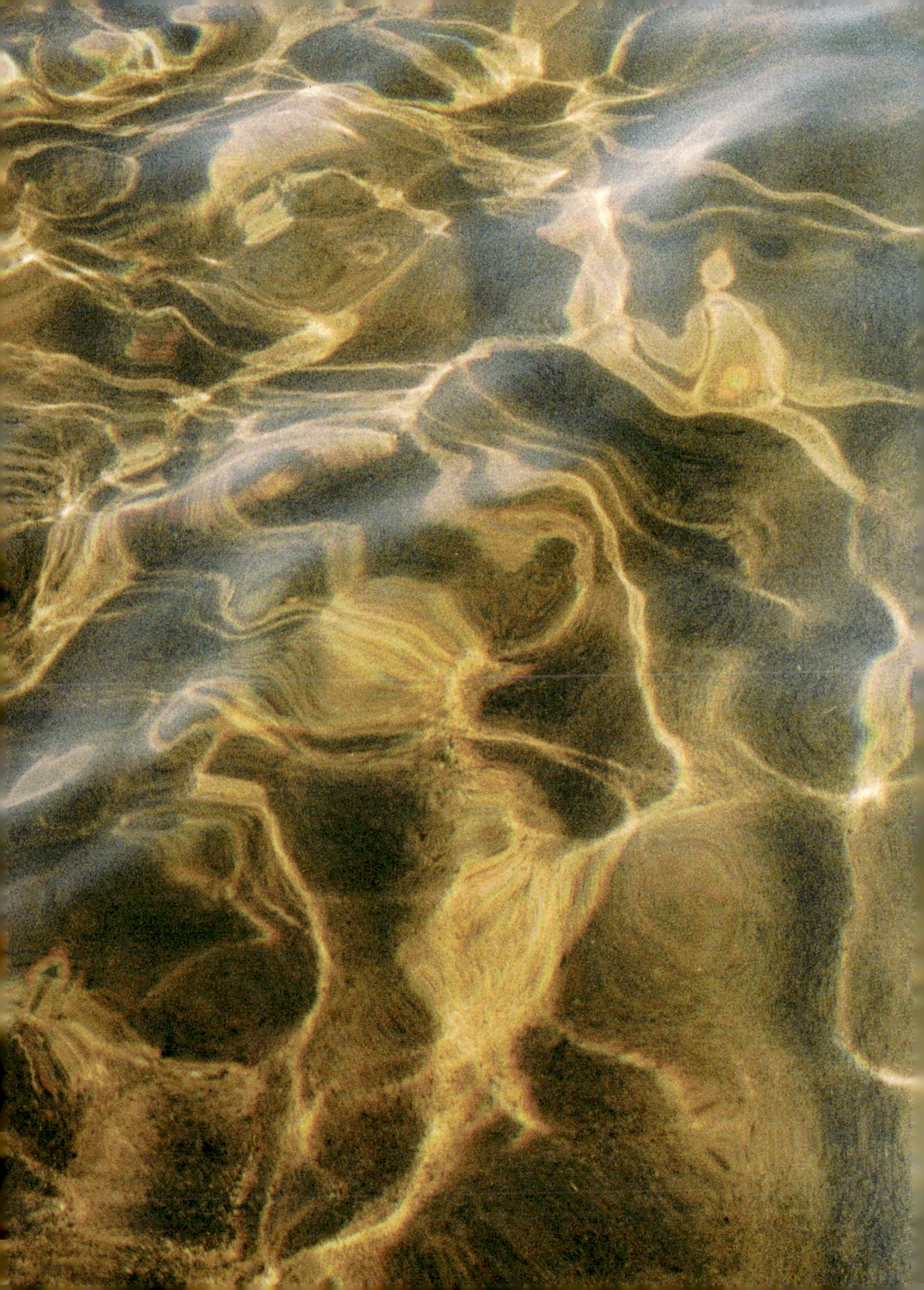

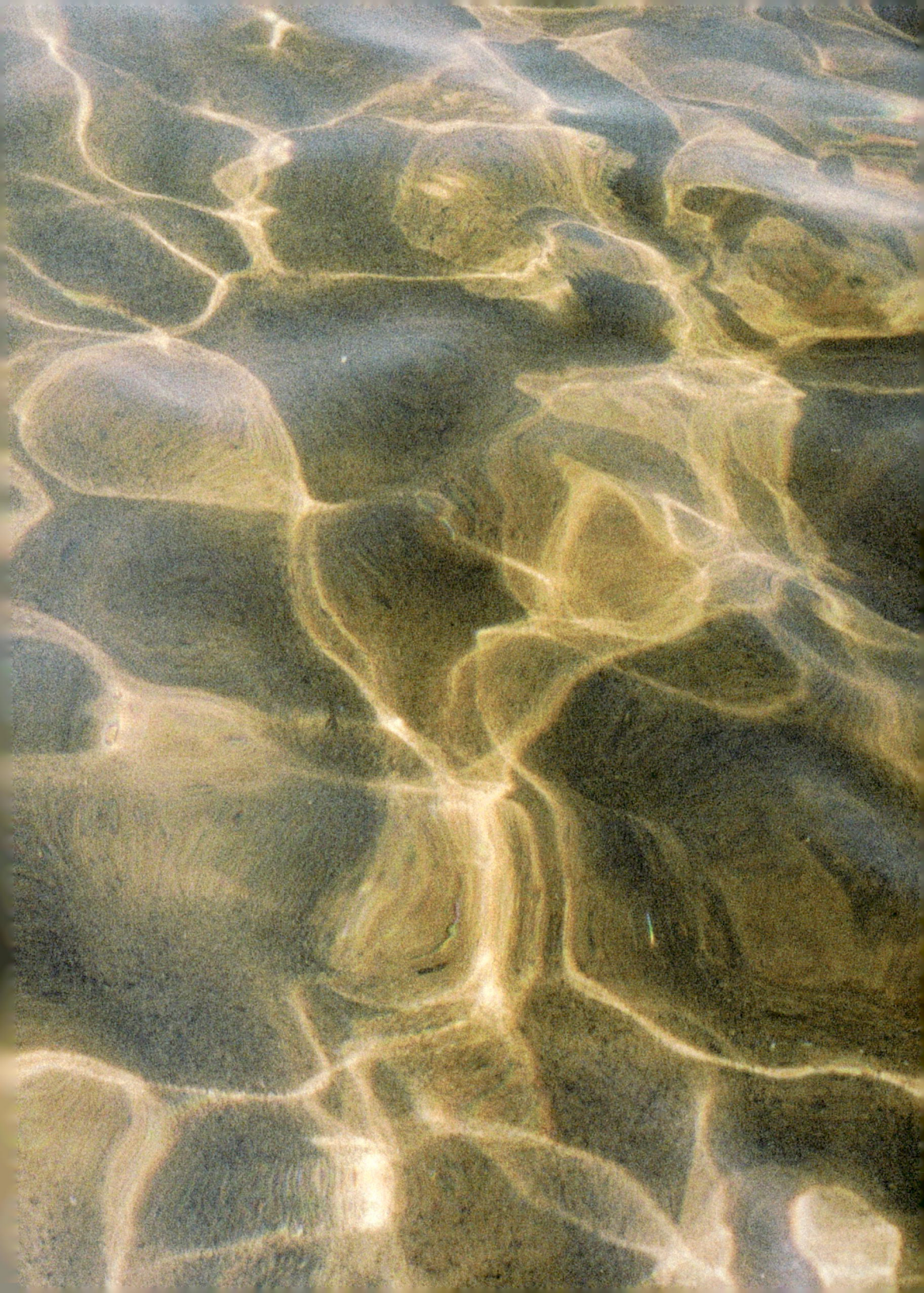

Dedication

To my grandchildren: Each time I am in their company, an overwhelming urge engulfs me—to impart to them the entirety of life's essential insights. They are so ready to learn, and I wish to convey our family's history, beliefs, values, and priorities, which they can share with generations to come.

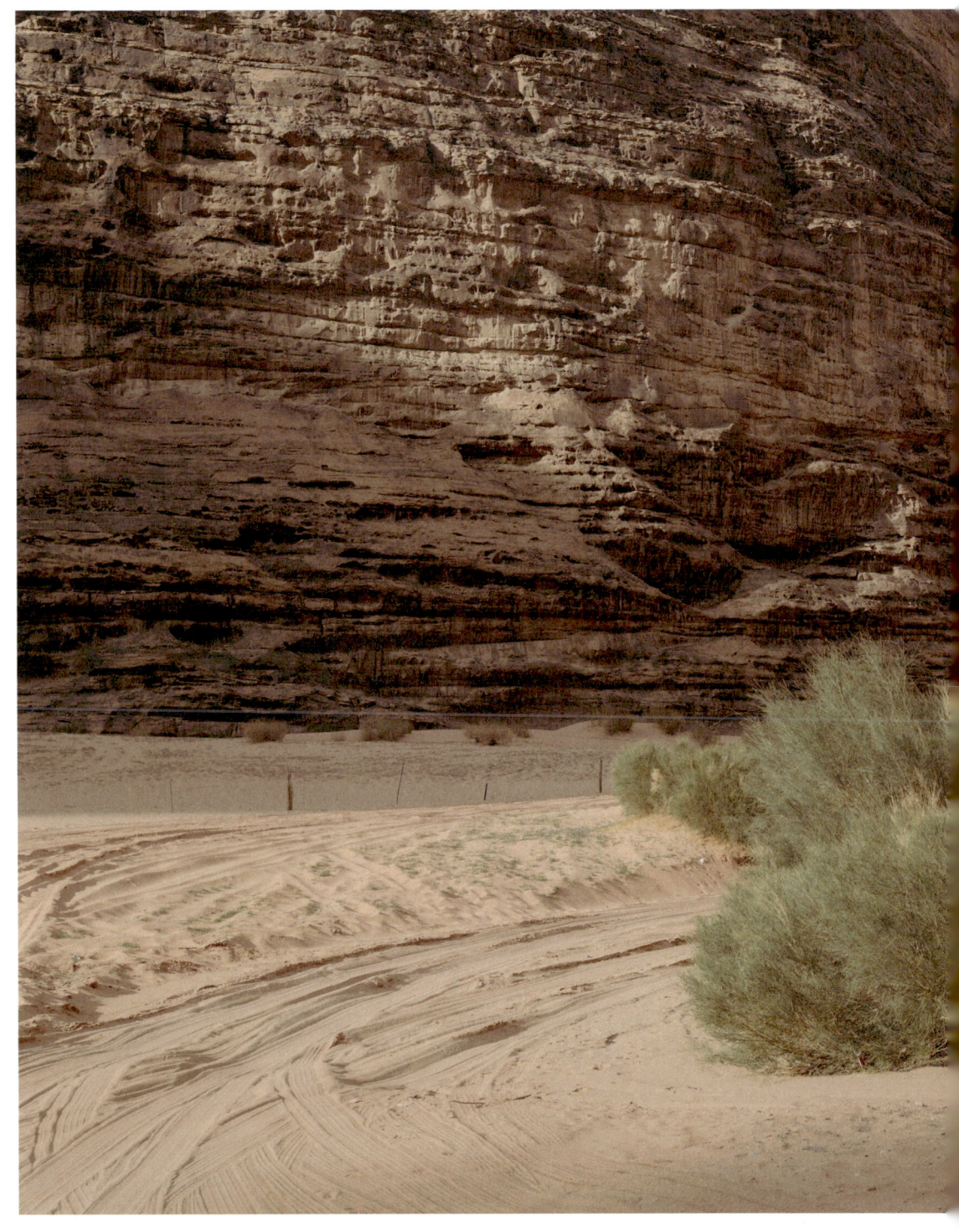

BEEN THERE, MYTHBUSTED THAT

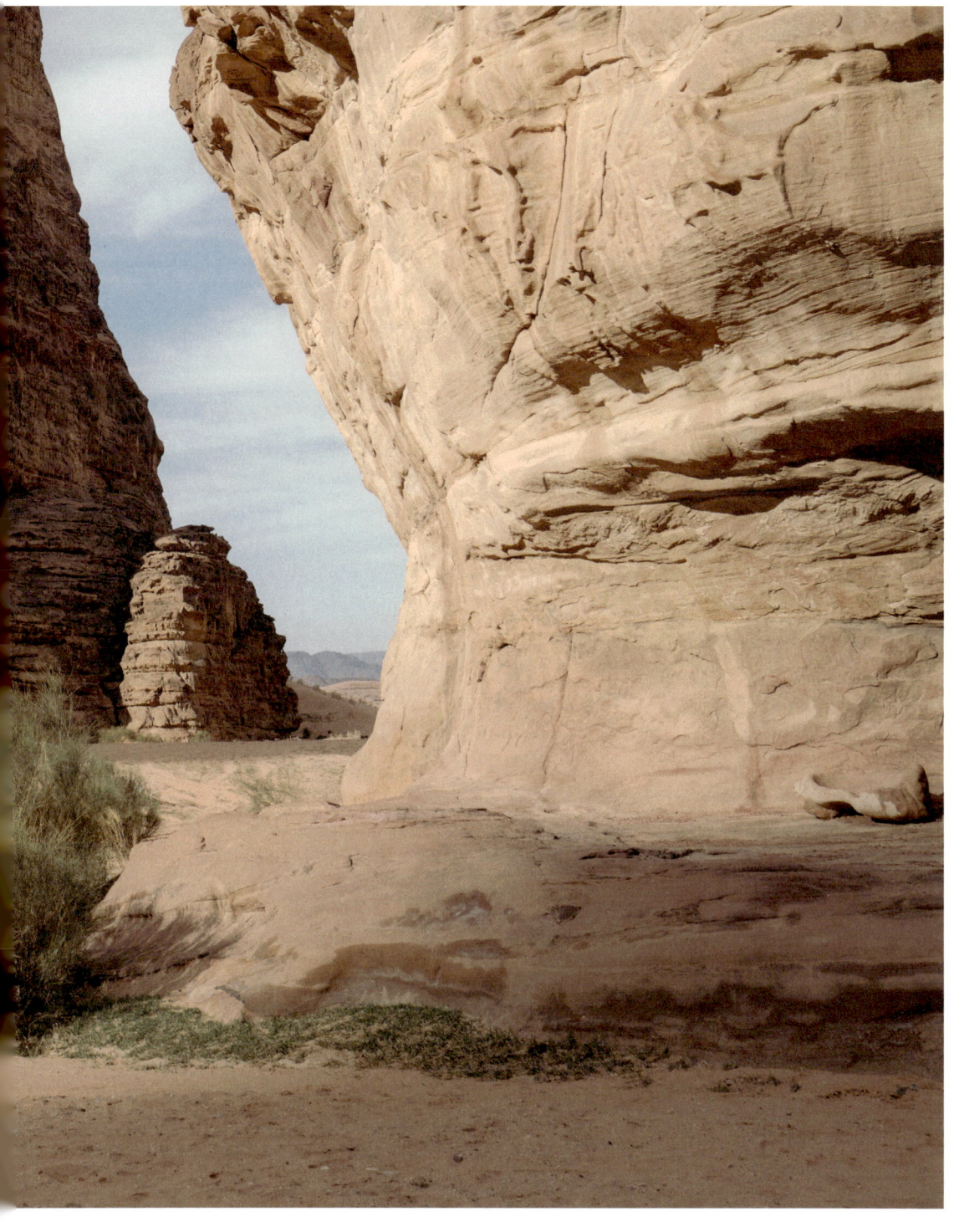

Prologue

The purpose of this book is to encourage others to continuously ask the question: *why?* We are beings constantly driven by superficial beliefs, reasonings, and justifications—but rarely do we peel back these layers and challenge our own ideologies.

Instead, we need to embark on a voyage of self-discovery: comprehending *why* we manifest in a certain manner, shaped by external influences from the moment of our birth. Please note that self-discovery is not self-help nor an endeavor to find oneself. During my coaching and mentoring sessions, my initial focus with students is to unravel hidden, subconscious factors. These latent influences can shackle an individual throughout their life, subtly dictating their choices without their conscious awareness. In this process, instead of me imposing a new belief system, it's about teaching how to uncover and question your unconscious belief system, and becoming more deliberate in developing a conscious belief system based on values that you truly embrace.

This book is arranged by chapter, with each challenging a conventional belief perpetuated by societal norms, education, tradition, and popular publications. But I caution; it's not meant to be a "self-help guide", nor prescriptive: I do not wish for you to emulate my beliefs. Instead, it is meant to challenge mainstream wisdom and prevailing trends, and present alternative worldviews: all in service of stimulating and stirring contemplation within yourself.

As you, my reader, journey through these pages, I urge you to scrutinize your motivations, be deliberate in your thoughts and actions, and foster a genuine concern for everything that you do. Embark on a journey of rethinking how to begin anew, akin to starting fresh on a pristine sheet of paper.

All proceeds of this book go to support my nonprofit UnCommon Voices Collective, a platform for uncommon voices in the world. *www.uncommonvoices.faith*

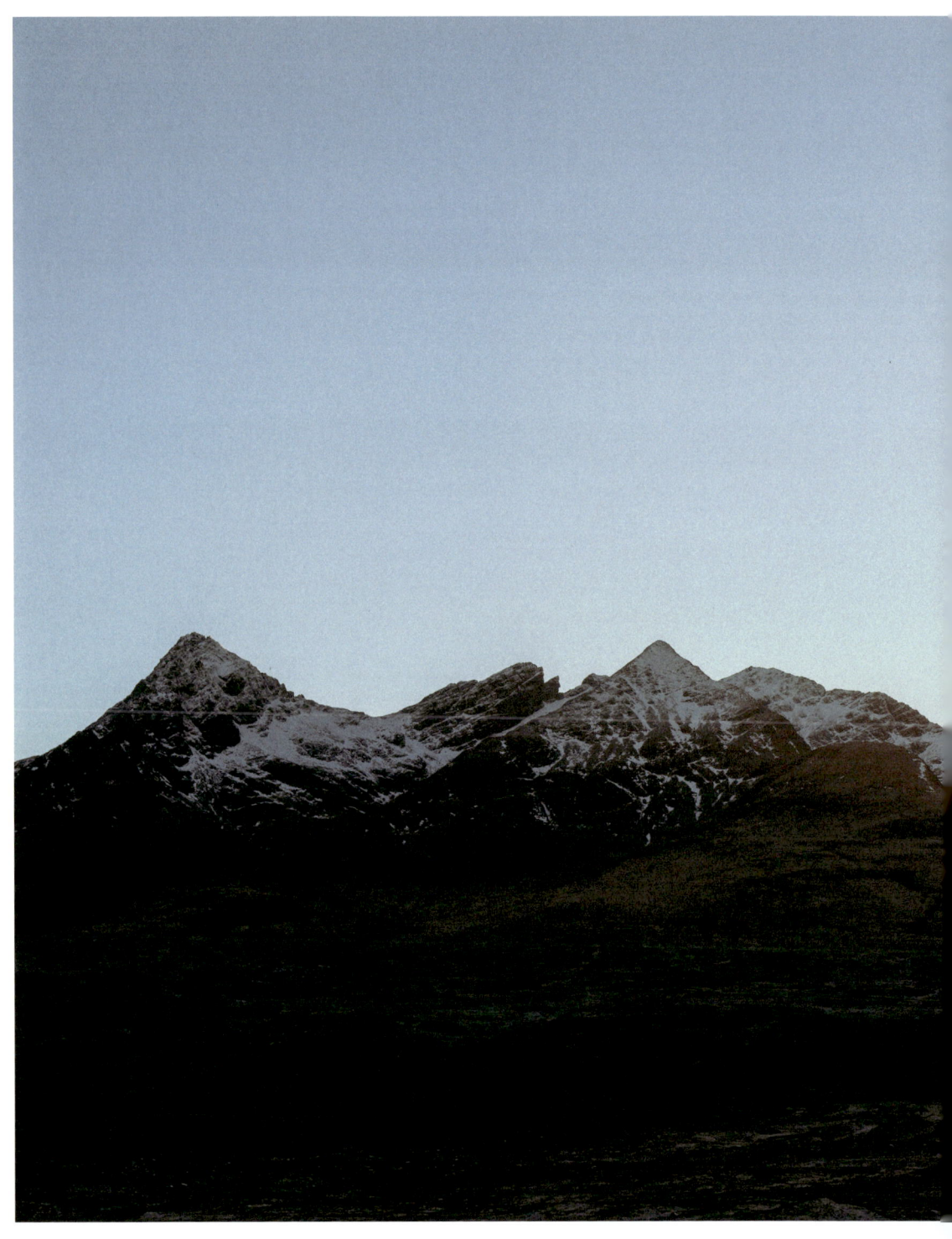

BEEN THERE, MYTHBUSTED THAT

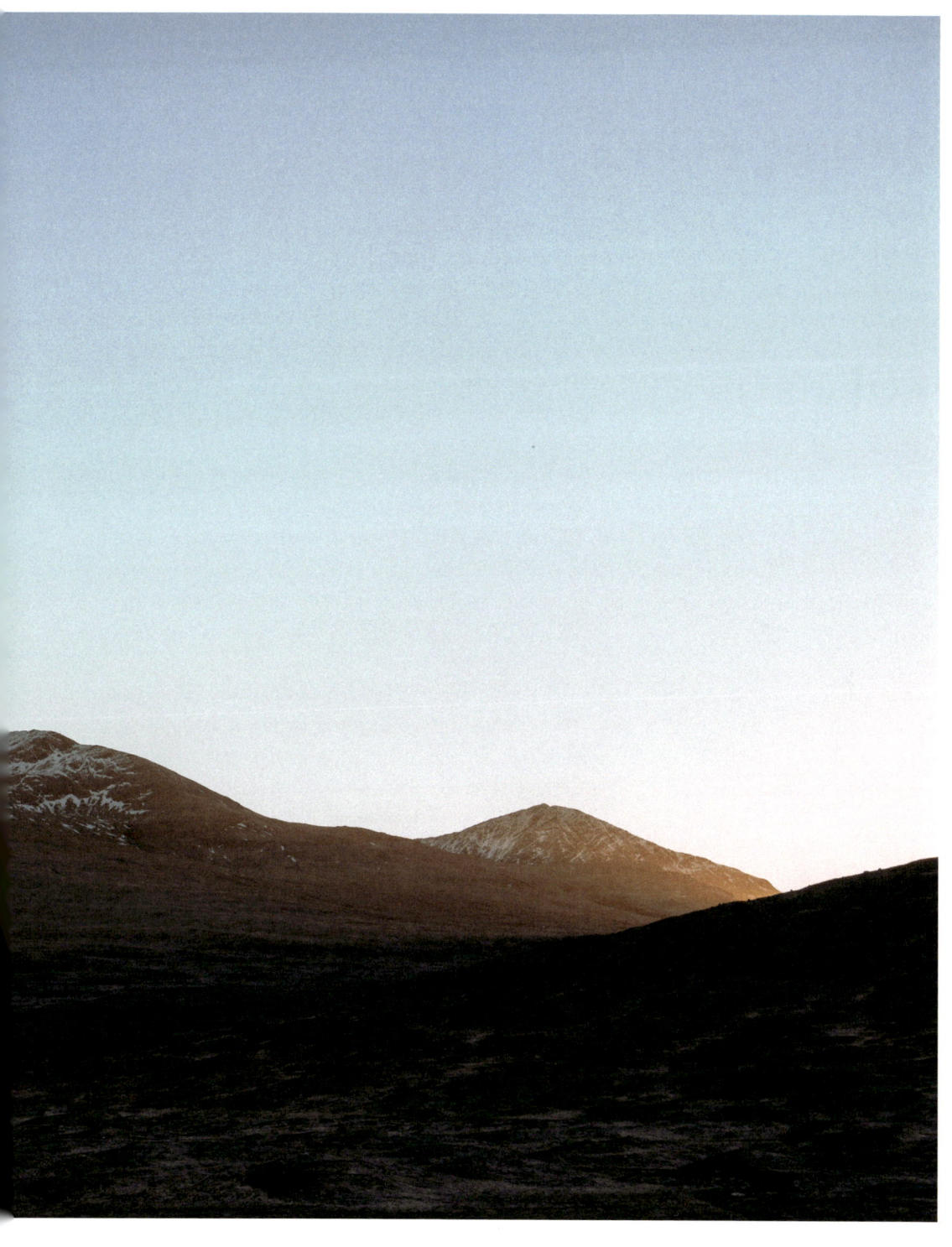

DANIEL FONG

Daniel Fong was born and raised in Hong Kong, where he attended Diocesan Boys' School, one of the top schools there. When he turned sixteen, he left Hong Kong to attend Worcester Academy, a boarding prep school in Massachusetts. He graduated as valedictorian and was accepted to Harvard. Thirty-seven years after graduating from Harvard, Daniel embarked on a Master of Arts in Theology degree at Fuller Theological Seminary in Pasadena, California, achieving it five years later.

Daniel worked first in Hong Kong for four years at one of the foremost denim fabrics manufacturing companies, which was owned by his father. Then, he joined Li & Fung Trading Limited, a multi-faceted global company. His work there included starting a private equity fund in San Francisco as well as creating the largest toy distribution network in Asia. When he was twenty-nine, he became the youngest Grade 1 director in their history.

In 1989, because of unsettling political events in Beijing, Daniel uprooted his young family and moved to Los Angeles. Shortly after, he bought a small baby furniture wholesaler, Million Dollar Baby, which has grown to become one of the premier companies in the industry. For the last eight years, he has been known there as Teacher/MythBuster. Additionally, Daniel is an investor and advisor at Alabaster Creative Inc., which sells beautiful Bible books, and is the founder of Uncommon Voices Collective, a nonprofit that lately has been focusing on Christian horror. It produced the Christian horror short film, *Refuse*; published the first Christian devotional based on eight horror stories from the Bible; co-created the podcast "Be Afraid" with Christianity Today and Fuller Theological Seminary; convened an in-person conference called FearMakers in 2023. He also sits on various boards and is particularly interested in helping needy students from Hong Kong go to US universities as well as finding solutions to help the unhoused population in Los Angeles.

Daniel has been married to his wife, Maryann, for forty-three years. He has a daughter, a son, and three grandchildren whom he adores.

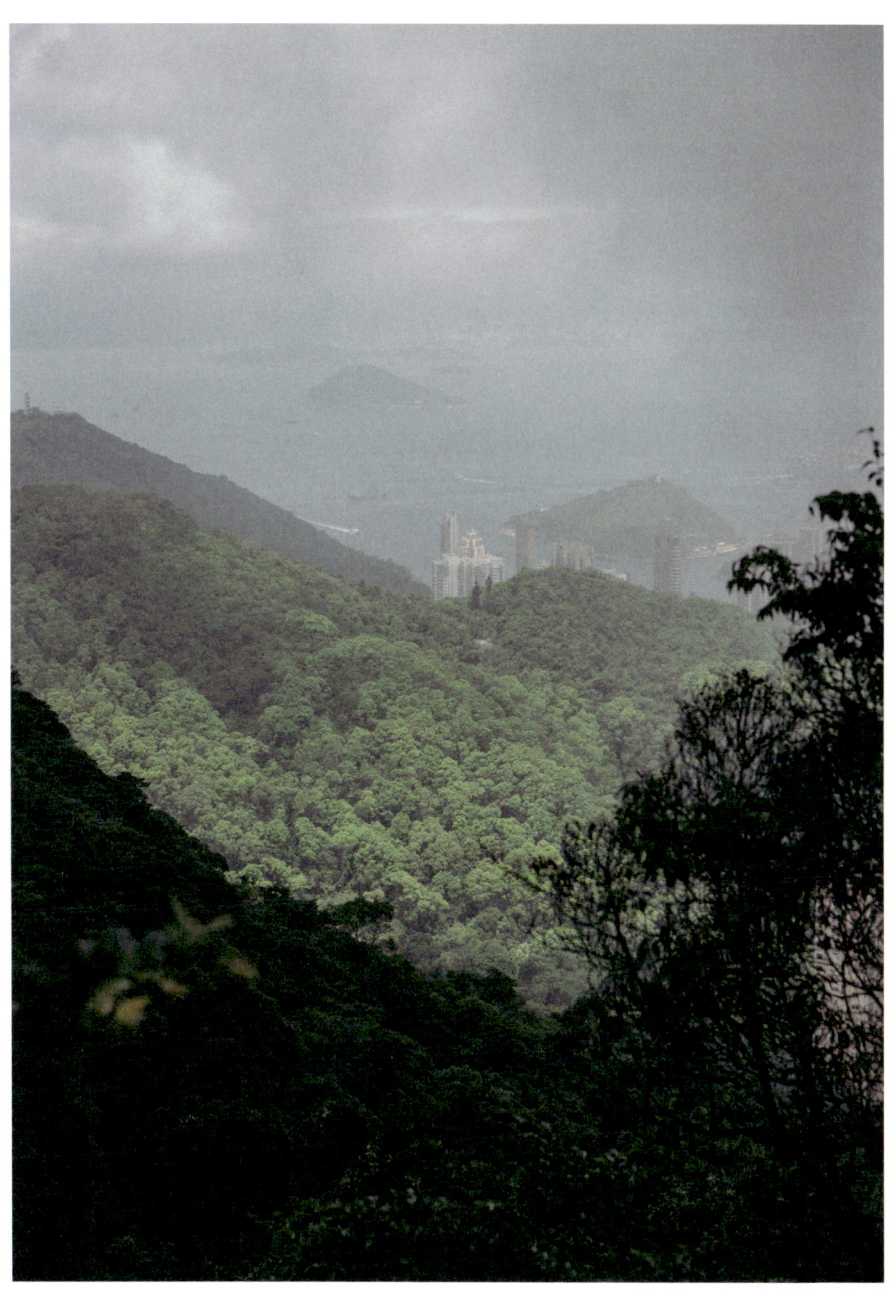

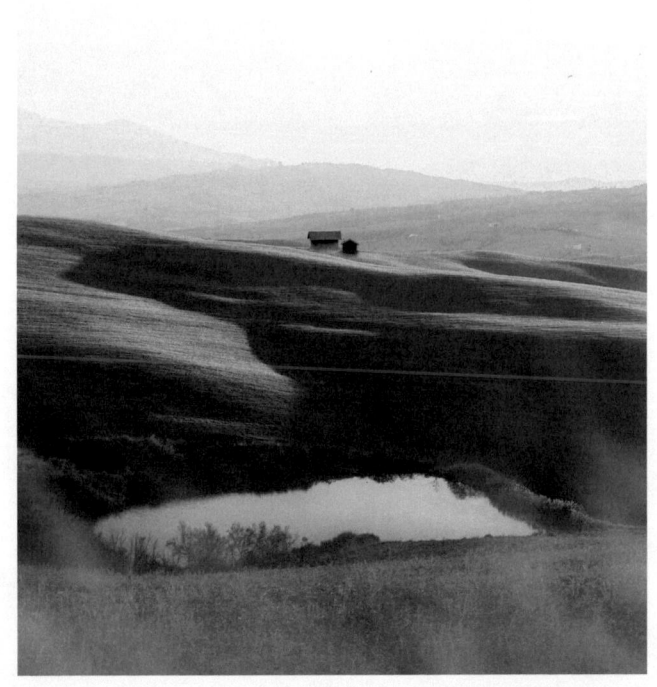

BEEN THERE, MYTHBUSTED THAT

Disclaimer

I am a serious follower of Jesus Christ, and I take great care in my choice of words. The term "Christian" originated in the first century after Jesus Christ's crucifixion and resurrection to describe his followers. Their distinct behavior set them apart, prompting the culture of that time to distinguish them from the general populace. However, the term "Christian" has acquired a negative connotation today, leading me to avoid using it. Instead, I prefer to identify myself as a serious follower of Jesus Christ, which I find to be a more fitting description. Research and polls indicate that while many people admire Jesus, they are skeptical about the religion of Christianity and its adherents.[1] I wholeheartedly share this perspective, as I believe organized religion has strayed from its original purpose, becoming more focused on personal glorification than the radical love that characterized the early Christians, especially toward those in dire need.

I share similar doubts about the current state of Christianity. Nevertheless, I have found that the teachings of Jesus Christ have provided me with the most constructive guidelines for living my life, conducting business, forming relationships, and gaining clarity about my identity and ongoing growth. It is, therefore, impossible for me to narrate my stories without acknowledging the source of my philosophies and the conclusions I have drawn thus far. Though this is the source of my narrative, I am not among those bestselling authors or speakers who claim to have "figured it all out" and offer motivational principles that appeal to the masses. Why? Because these purveyors cater to our desire for control, eliminating uncertainties and mysteries in life—feeding our can-do mentality. Some self-proclaimed successful

---

1: *https://www.episcopalchurch.org/jesus-in-america/*

leaders, heroes, or role models, having achieved recognition, believe they possess unique methods or programs for success. Their mission is to teach others to replicate their success. I, too, was once a disciple of these writers and speakers. During that phase, I consumed their content wholeheartedly, treating their teachings as the essence of life, indispensable and vital for my future success. As I matured and delved deeper into Jesus Christ's teachings, I began to discern the gaps and recognize that what sounded enticing was often too good to be true.

Over time, I evolved into a more discerning reader, critically assessing and identifying the myths propagated by these bestselling figures. This shift coincided with my transition from being a CEO in 2015 to embracing a role as a teacher and mythbuster. In my view, this tactic of claiming to know the "correct way" is one of the strategies employed by the Devil to divert our focus from Jesus Christ's teachings and redirect it towards ourselves and our egos. Another tactic is to keep us perpetually busy by accelerating the pace of change in our world. By being busy all the time, we lack the discipline to think deeply and, instead, we react subconsciously in a continuous autopilot mode.

My primary objective is to elucidate how my faith or theology serves as the foundation of my existence, guiding my thoughts, decisions, and actions. I have no intention of evangelizing or employing this book to persuade you to believe in Jesus Christ—let me be unequivocally clear about this. My theology doesn't impose upon me the responsibility to save or convince any of you to embrace Jesus Christ. That task belongs to the Holy Spirit. My role is that of a witness and storyteller, sharing how I live my life through the guidance of the indwelling Holy Spirit. I trust that, upon reading this book or perhaps encountering me personally in the future, you will recognize the distinctiveness of my life and perhaps understand that it stems from following a different role model or leader. In essence, you might gain insight into why the early followers of Jesus Christ were referred to as Christians.

At its core, the goal of this book lies in myth busting. It is not about delineating right from wrong. My focus lies solely on what embodies love and goodness. While right and wrong foster opposing positions, love and goodness embrace unity.

Many Christians are familiar with the Bible verse attributed to the Apostle Paul when he wrote to Christians in Rome, recorded in Romans 12. It reads, "Do not conform to the pattern of this world, but be transformed by the renewing of your mind. Then you will be able to test and approve what God's will is—His good, pleasing, and perfect will."

Most people interpret it as a warning not to conform to the pattern of this world. However, it is crucial to recognize that we are already conforming to the world, and we need to stop, think, review, and realize that we are heading in the wrong direction. Only then can we turn toward truth. This is the root meaning of repentance. To me, following the myths that I have identified is tantamount to conforming to the pattern of this world. Allow me to help you change that.

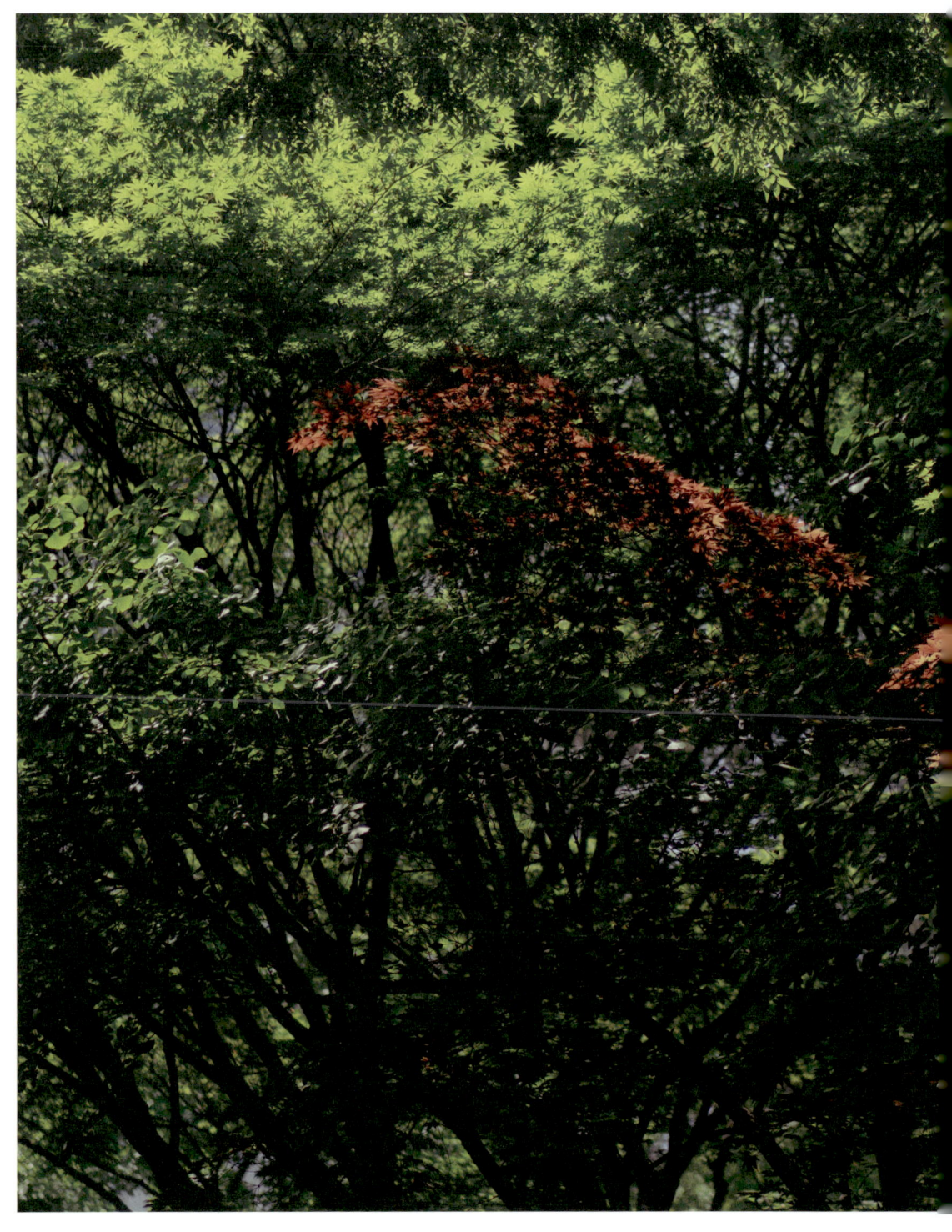

BEEN THERE, MYTHBUSTED THAT

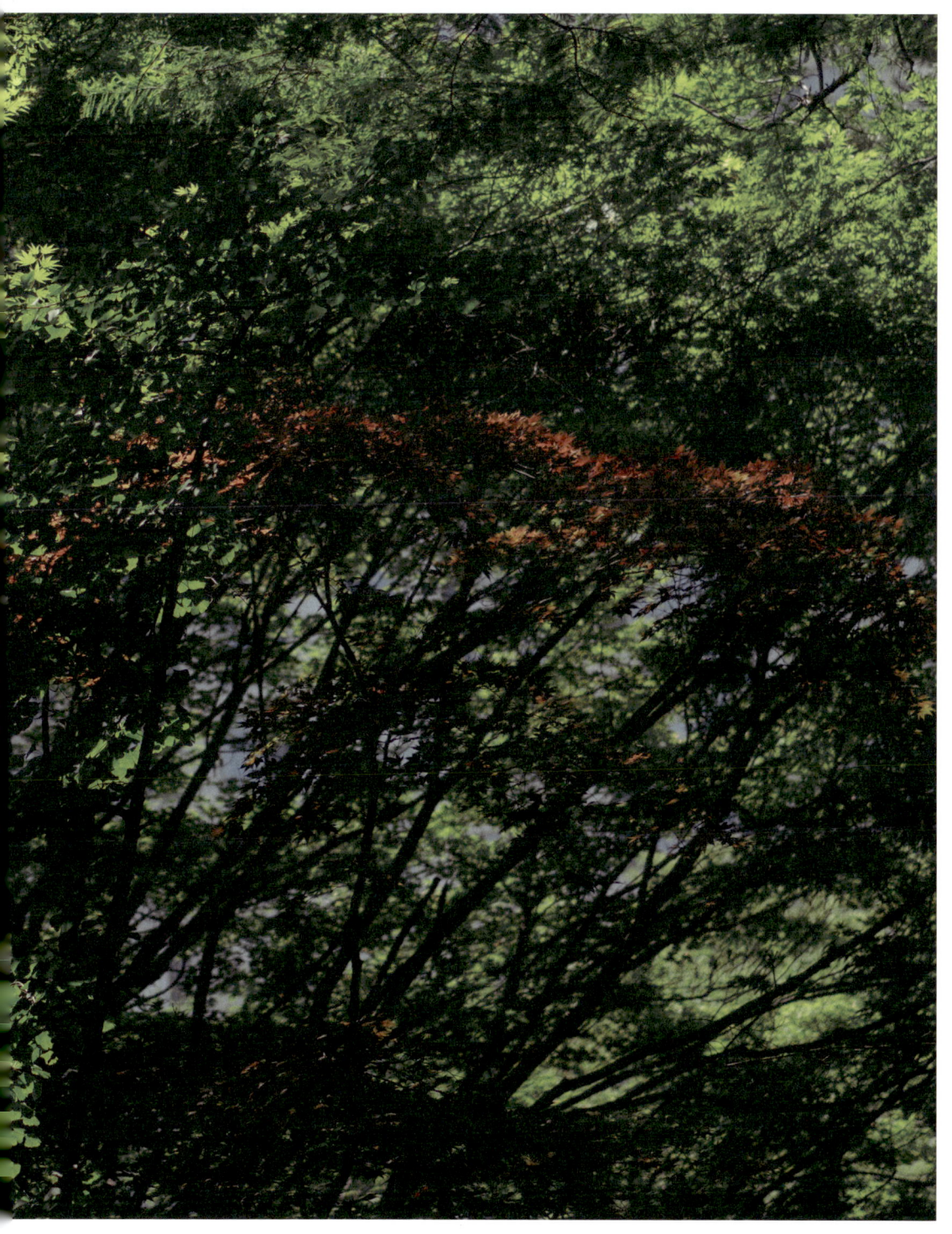

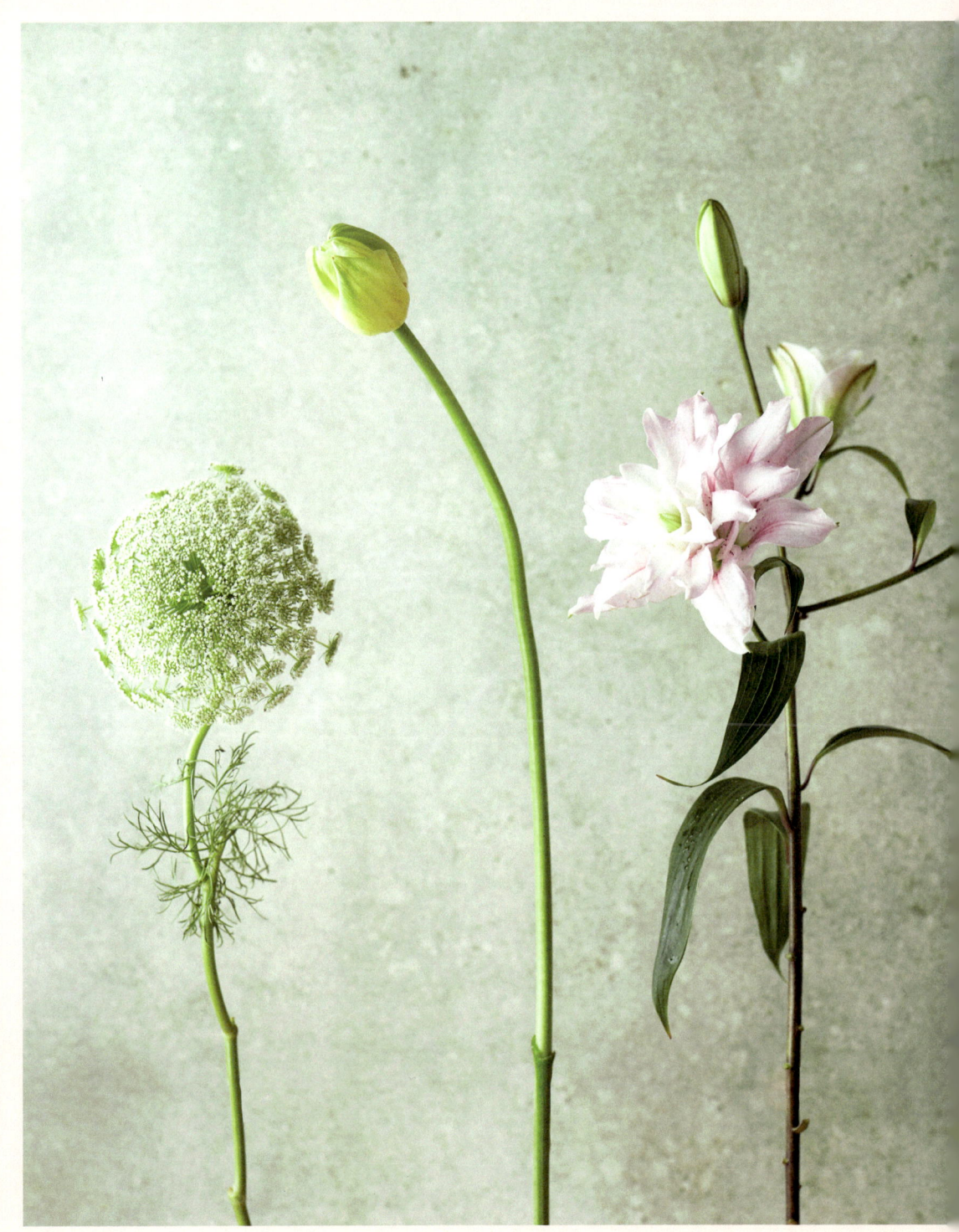

BEEN THERE, MYTHBUSTED THAT

Myth

LIFE IS COMPARTMENTALIZED TO BUSINESS, PLEASURE, AND SPIRITUAL

LIVE A COMPREHENSIVE AND INTEGRATED LIFE

Are you traveling for business or leisure? Most people I know tend to categorize their journeys in this way. In 1983, I commenced my business-related travels upon joining Li & Fung Trading Company in Hong Kong. This phenomenon of sorting into business versus leisure can be described as compartmentalized living. In the context of Christianity, Sundays hold a significant place as a time dedicated to one's spiritual life. For a number of years, I indeed led a compartmentalized life in this manner. While I did occasionally reunite with friends and family members during business trips, it was only after I started traveling with my wife, Mary-ann, that I began to seamlessly integrate business and pleasure.

The transition to this integrated approach took place in 1997 when my son left home to attend Milton Academy, a boarding school located just outside Boston, joining his older sister and a cousin. Consequently, my wife and I, now empty nesters, have been traveling together for more than twenty-six years. This has rendered the artificial division of our travels into business or pleasure essentially meaningless. Upon our return from trips, even from close friends, we are often asked about the nature of our travels, whether they are for business or leisure. Now, I respond, "We work for pleasure, and pleasure is our work." In addition, since my work and travels involve my faith in Jesus Christ, our trips are spiritual in nature also. That is why I am not reorganizing my chapters into three different books as suggested by one editor. His observation is that most books are organized around the three most popular categories of personal, business, and spiritual and that maybe organizing my advice into these three categories would help with sales.

After carefully considering the editor's advice, I made the decision to challenge a significant misconception regarding living a compartmentalized life, portraying it as unfulfilling. Instead, I advocate for the concept of leading a fully integrated and holistic life, which allows individuals to experience a less stressful existence rooted in a belief system or theology that permeates every facet of their lives, without creating artificial distinctions or separations. Thus, instead of three different books, the subject became my first myth.

One practical application of this philosophy involves incorporating various elements into activities such as business trips. By consciously allocating time before and after the trip to connect with friends and family or explore historical sites to gain a deeper understanding of their stories and cultures, we can transform each journey into an opportunity for personal growth and enrichment. Have you ever considered it? This approach not only enhances our knowledge and learning but also fosters stronger connections with friends and family members, nurturing our closest relationships after spending time with business partners. Take vacation days from your business if that is what it will take for you to adopt this transformational new way of traveling.

At Million Dollar Baby, we pay our employees to go on vacations. For international travel, the annual subsidy is $1,000. For a while after we started the practice almost twenty years ago, employees would offer a travel presentation at our quarterly performance review meeting and share with the entire company their learnings and recommendations on how we can all practice continuous learning and continuous improvement, one of the core values at Million Dollar Baby. In that sense, aren't we integrating positive business elements into our employees' vacation travels?

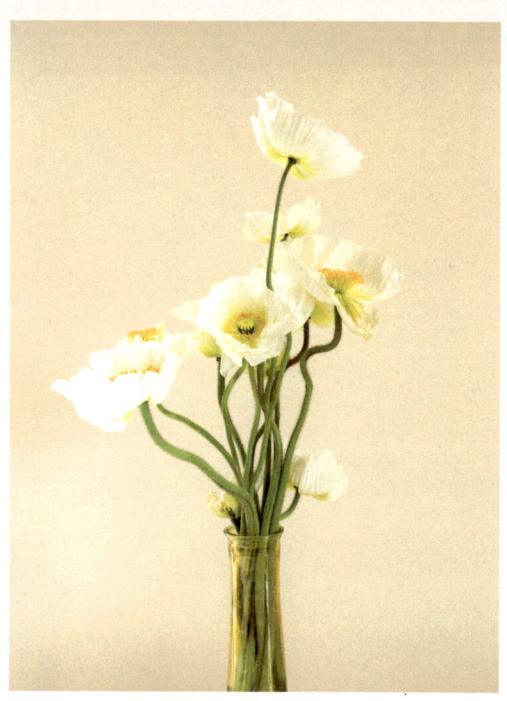

ty of our overall life. For example, the outcome of a particular business call may, in fact, affect whether there will be any more holidays in the future. As I have stated before, I am not trying to be prescriptive. My intention is to stimulate thought and prompt readers to ask questions that they may not have asked themselves before.

To me, there are many myths disguised as conventional wisdom or widely adopted practices that most people go through life without ever questioning. It is my intention to encourage you to be intentional about living instead of going through life guided by subconscious beliefs that should actually be reviewed and challenged continuously.

I can understand the pushback from many of you regarding why it is so important to keep vacations sacred with no interruptions from business activities. In that sense, why shouldn't we keep our leisure time compartmentalized? From my own experience, the issue is more a practice of setting priorities or time blocking so that we can have uninterrupted time for certain tasks that require our full attention. This form of compartmentalization is not in conflict with my promotion of a mindset of living an integrated and comprehensive life. In other words, as long as I am present and set clear priorities, just having a business call should not cause trauma to the rest of the holiday trip. Besides, a business call can have an impact on the quali-

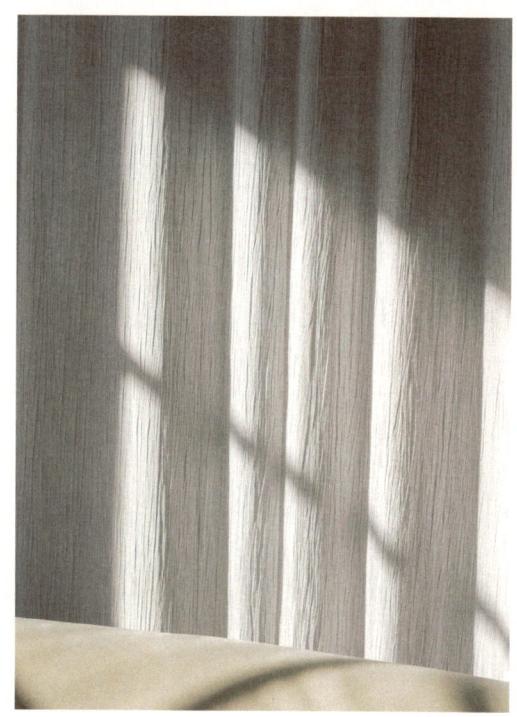

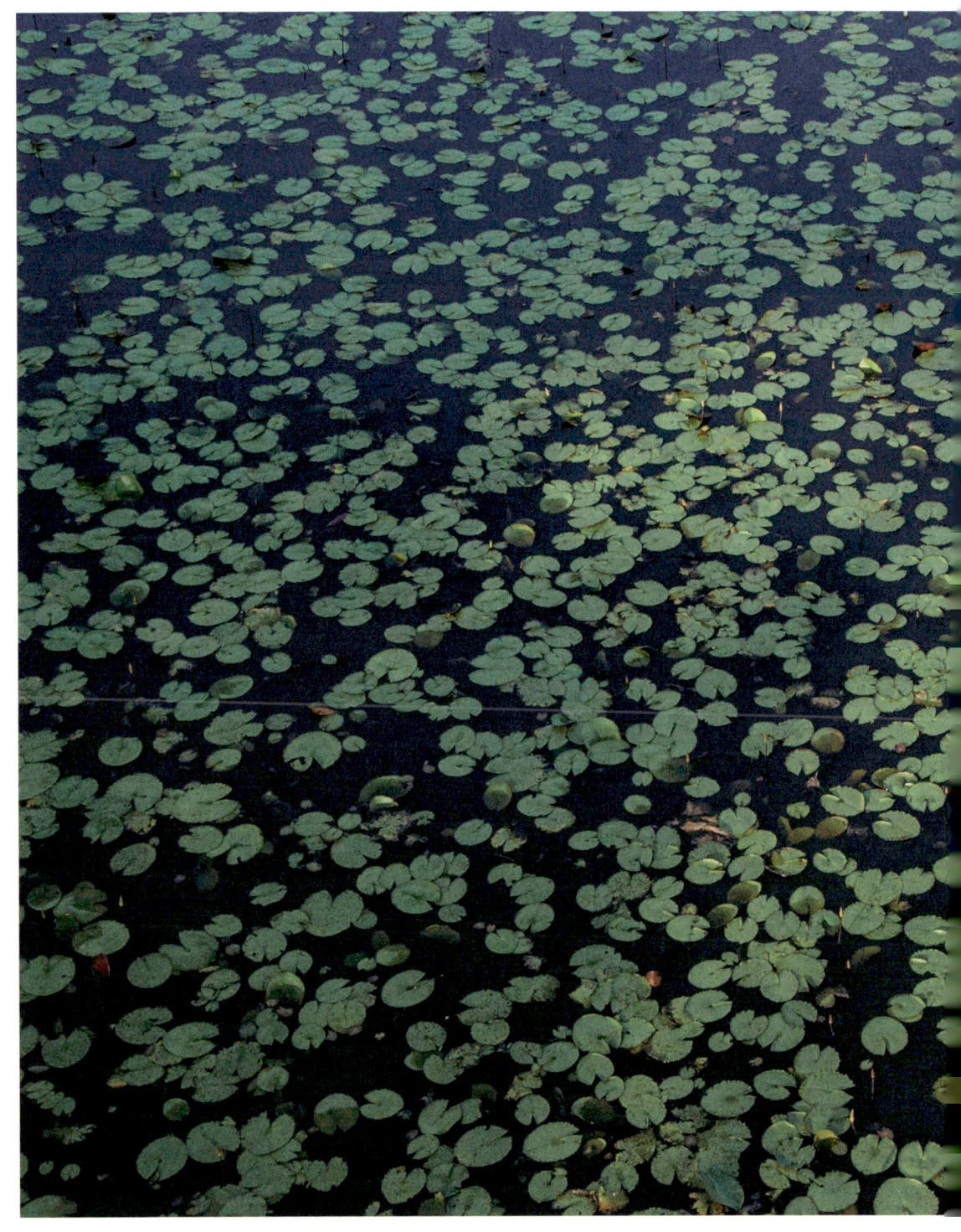

BEEN THERE, MYTHBUSTED THAT

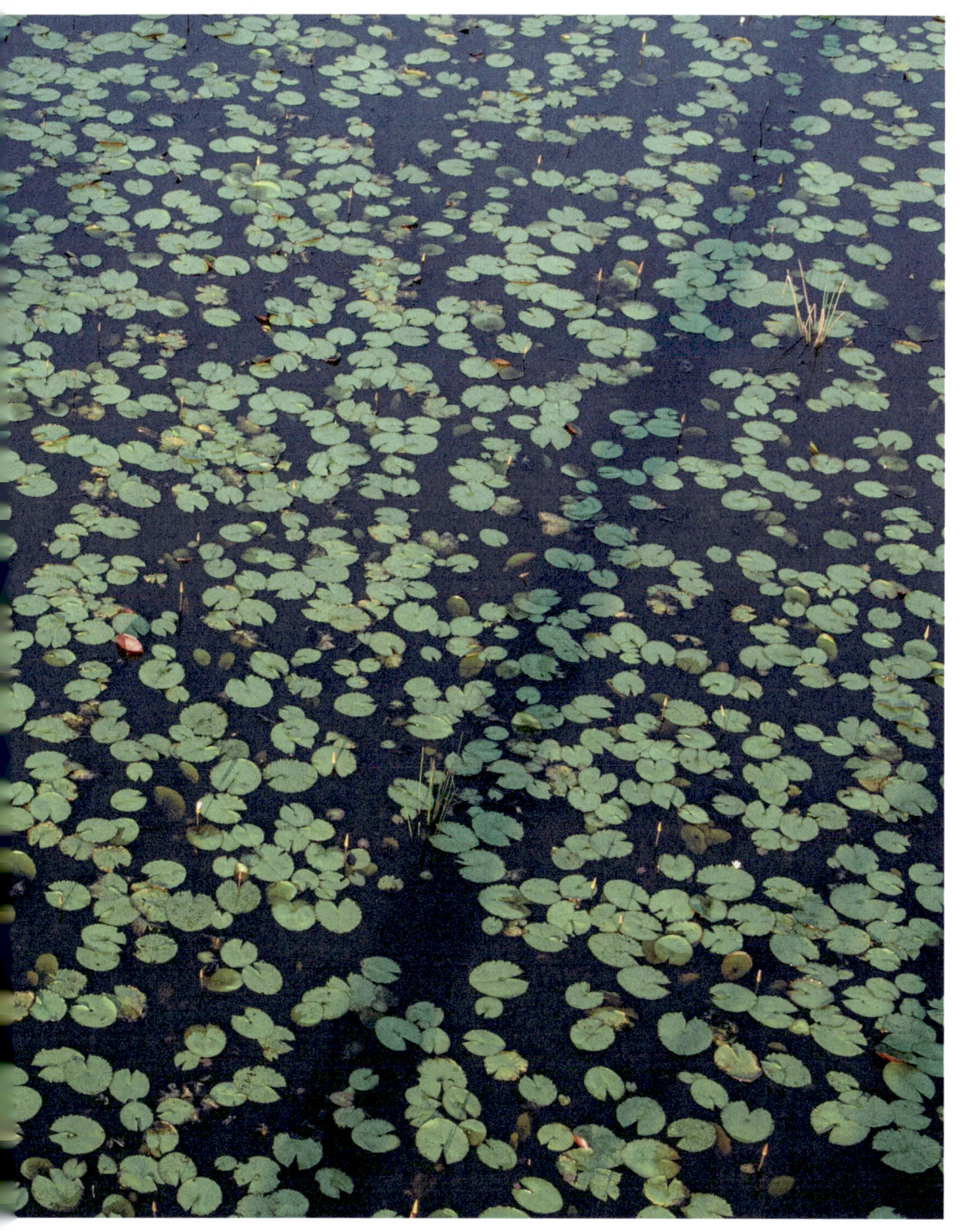

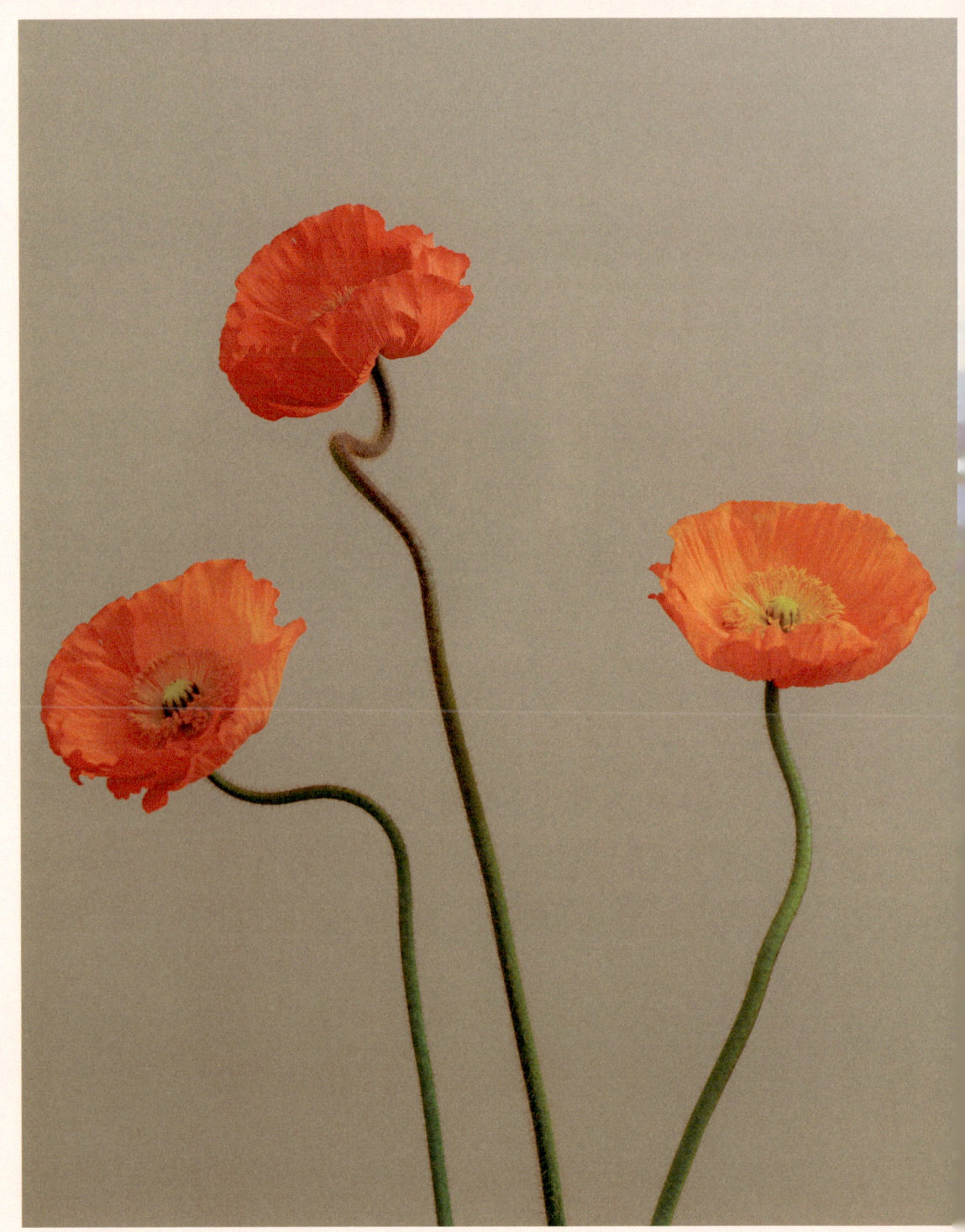

BEEN THERE, MYTHBUSTED THAT

Myth

A FULL LIFE = EVERYTHING, ALL THE TIME

Truth
EMBRACE THE SEASON OF LIFE

It is crucial to accept and appreciate the concept of life having various seasons. Failing to grasp that these changing seasons symbolize ongoing transformations in both life and the universe can lead to anxiety and disappointment.

An example of how that anxiety manifests at Christian colleges is when seniors worry about what they will do after graduation. More often than not, they consider becoming a missionary to be the highest "calling." Pursuing one's interest and learning is secondary, and working for a for-profit business is the lowest option. Their anxiety peaks, as if they are deciding their one and only career for the rest of their lives.

That is where I inject the reality of seasons in life. Our life on earth is temporal, and so are our careers. There really is no such thing as a lifelong pursuit anymore due to the rapid changes happening all around us. It is a different world from a hundred years ago—and it will be very different a hundred years from now. The seasons in life doctrine is to respect and live according to the seasons in our lives.

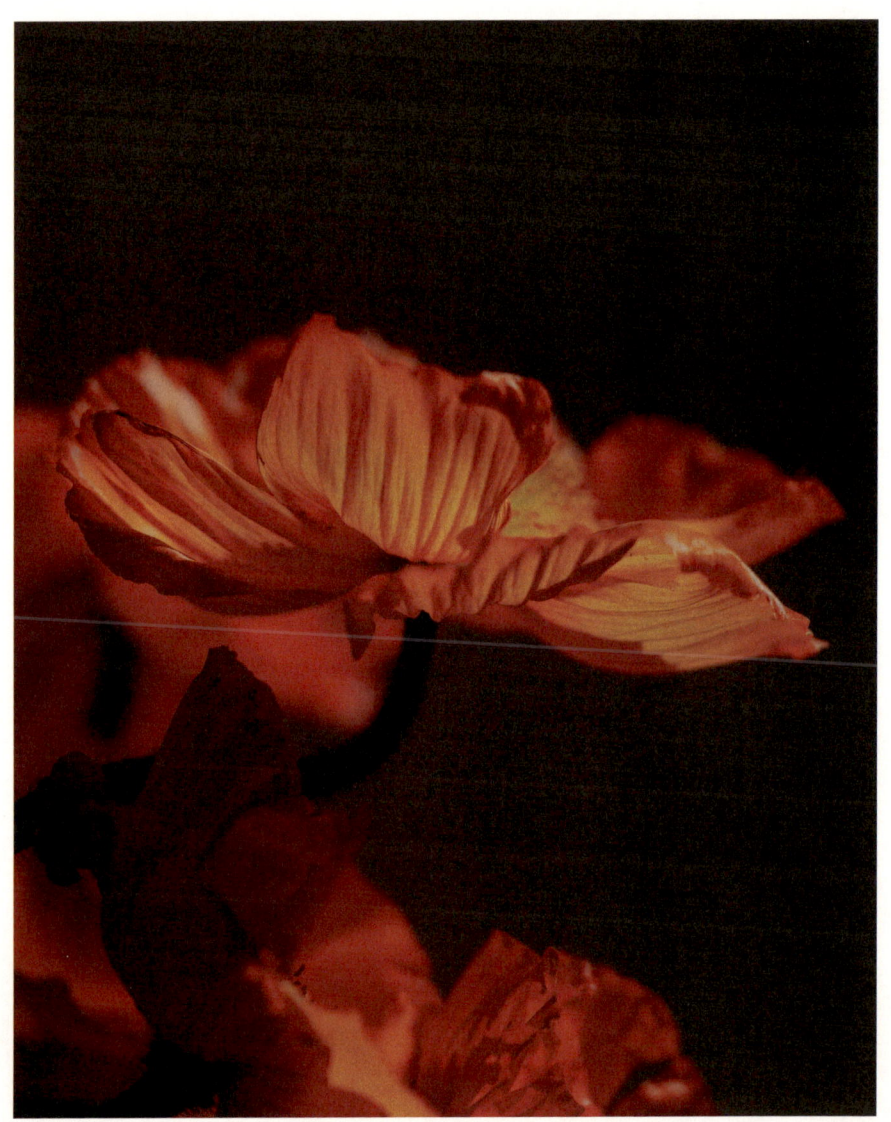

BEEN THERE, MYTHBUSTED THAT

Another example is how young parents struggle with the transition from being single, then married with no children, to the life-changing event of having a child. The complete change in schedule and priorities stands in stark contrast to the freedom the couple once enjoyed. My advice to them is to embrace the season of child-rearing as a fifteen-year season per child. After the fifteen-year child-rearing season, your child is in the season of adulthood—they can begin making some decisions on their own—and the season to look forward to next is the season of empty nesting.

The season doctrine can be applied to a more general understanding that there is a time for everything, and we should recognize each season and then live accordingly. It is how I live daily. I view time periods during the day as seasons, and I will act according to the season that I think I am in.

Ultimately, the season doctrine is about respecting the various seasons in our life. It is not about "repeating" seasons throughout our lives but encourages us to keep moving with every "new" season.

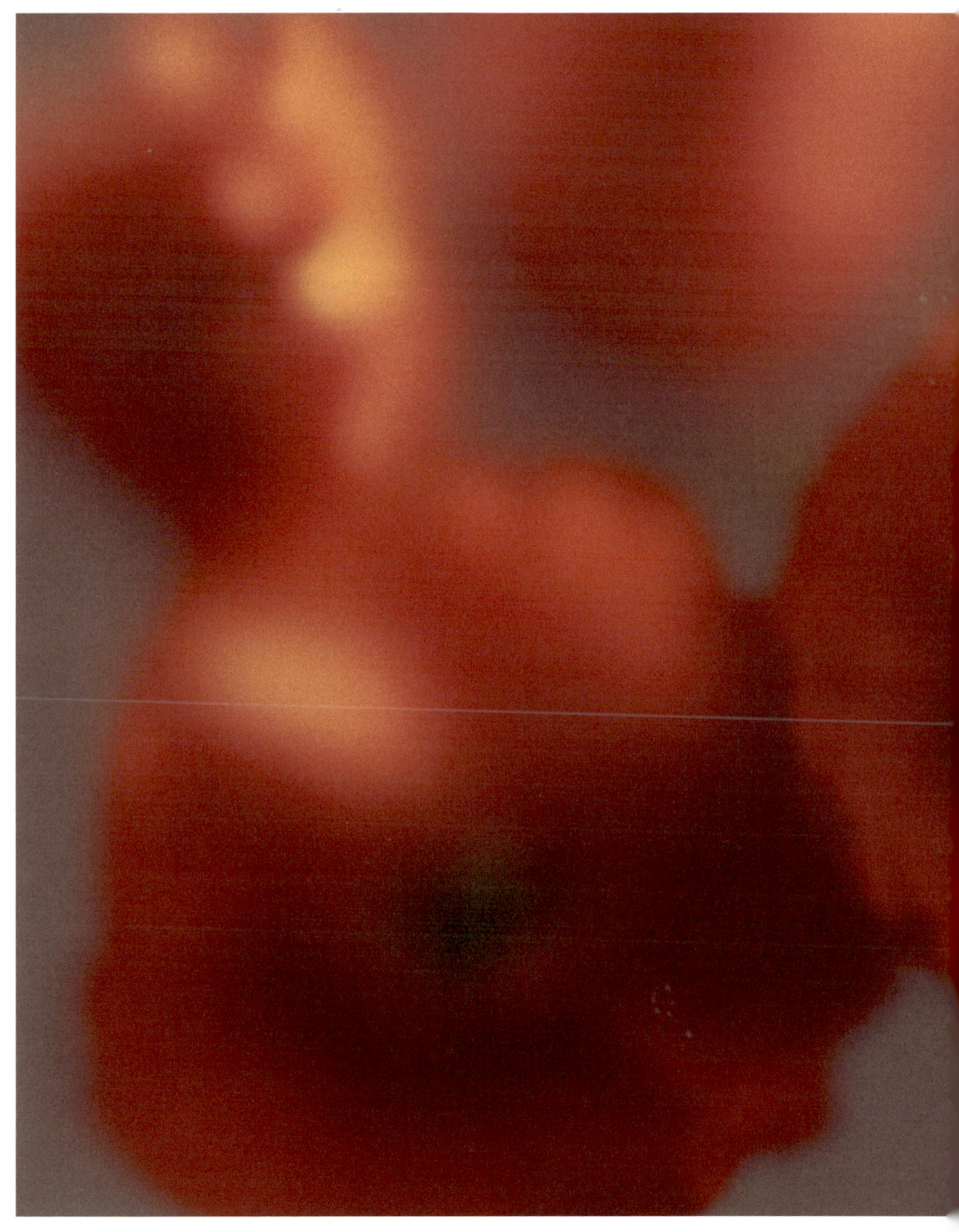

BEEN THERE, MYTHBUSTED THAT

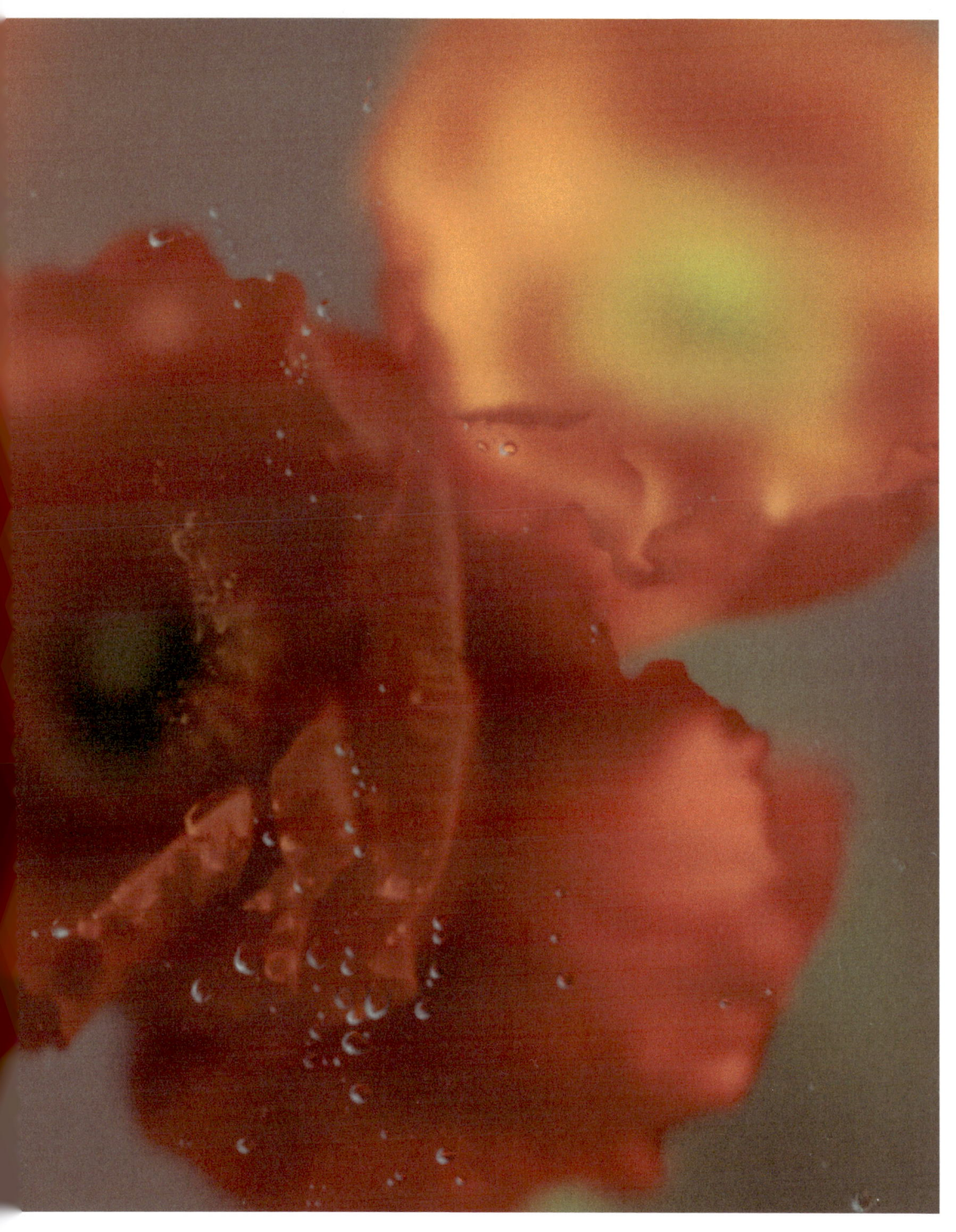

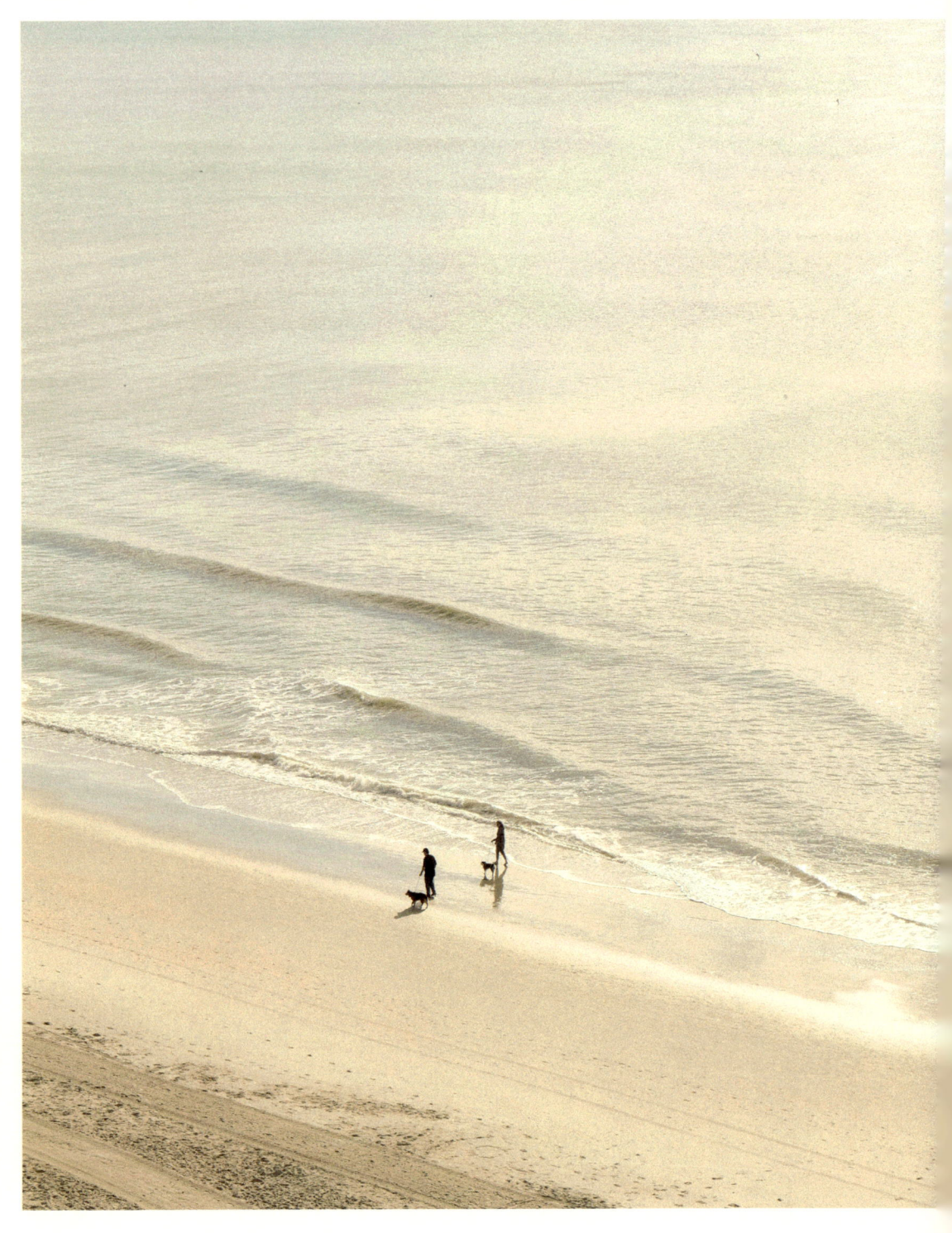

BEEN THERE, MYTHBUSTED THAT

Myth

MY PARENTS ARE
MY BEST FRIENDS

Truth
MY PARENTS ARE MY BEST FATHER AND MOTHER

I advise young parents to be their children's best parent instead of being their best friend, especially during the first fifteen years of the child's life. It is a myth that I have noticed in weddings with the bride or groom identifying their parents as their best friend. Should all parents strive to be their children's best friend? Why not strive to be their best parent? Naming your parents as best friends is not an apt replacement for declaring that the parents are not judgmental. I would rather be the best parent to my children and the best grandparent to my grandchildren. Let your best friend be your best friend!

The flip side of the coin is also important. Shouldn't our children also strive to be our best children instead of our best friend? I have seen many of my friends struggle with their children living in other states or countries, and they share with me how much they miss their grandchildren. Instead of going into a deep discourse, I will just ask why moving away from family for the sake of work would be an unquestionable and automatic priority for most families. If you are an only child and have aging parents, instead of working close to your parents, why would working out of state or out of the country be an expression of your divine role to be the best child possible?

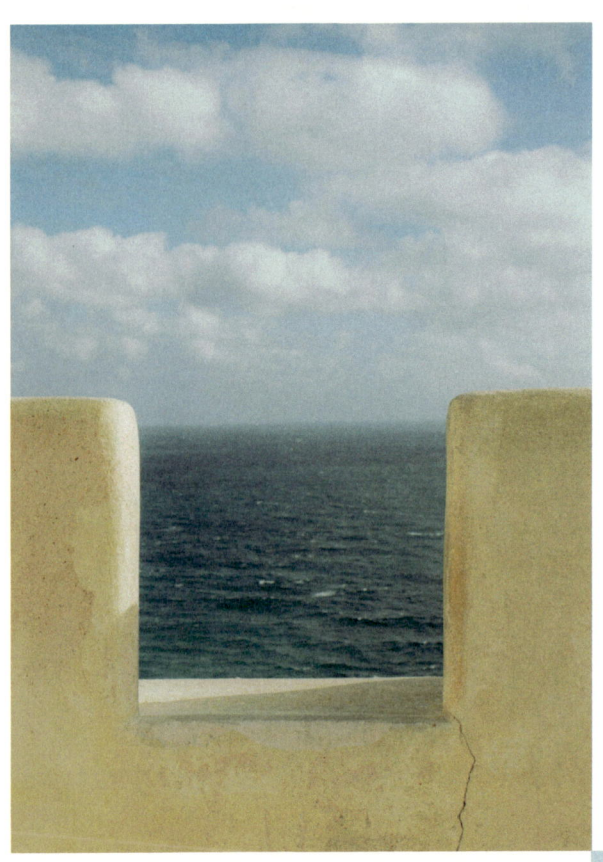

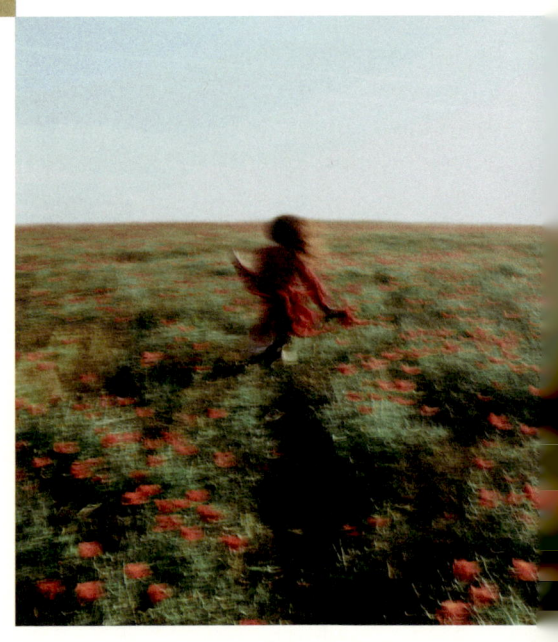

BEEN THERE, MYTHBUSTED THAT

My wife, Maryann, and I took great responsibilities in raising our two children to be positive contributors to our fallen world. If our children make mistakes, we do not want to blame the school, society, our community, or circumstances except our own negligence. Therefore, we set clear and strict boundaries for our children and practice "deregulation" when our children demonstrate maturity in making their own decisions. In other words, our children, when growing up, were not allowed to make any decisions until they have proven otherwise. For example, they ate whatever Maryann and I decided that they should eat and with no leftovers. They never stayed overnight at their friends' homes while their friends were welcomed to stay at ours. By sending my children to boarding schools, it made the decision not to allow them to drive a car until after college much easier. I told them that I totaled my first two cars after college and, based on my disastrous track record, I didn't believe that they should drive when they were teenagers. Some of my friends actually asked us if we love our children when we sent them off to boarding school for their high school education; they, instead, restrict their children to only local universities in the Los Angeles area. That is why I repeatedly clarify that I am not selling a formula, nor a self help book. There is no method to be an excellent parent, only a desire and a focus. The myth I am trying to bust is that being the best parent is the same as being your children's best friend.

So, instead of giving you a clear plan, recognize that all parents are different and all children are different; therefore, every relationship is different and needs to be customized. Since there is no formula, we must embrace the process of continuous learning and continuous improvement. It is an intentional process because, from my observations and conclusions, all issues of younger generations are caused by older generations. It is easy to blame the younger generation when we never inspect how we, the older generation, are the cause.

Continuous improvement is the reality that we all are born with a blank sheet of paper and must acquire our knowledge through learning.

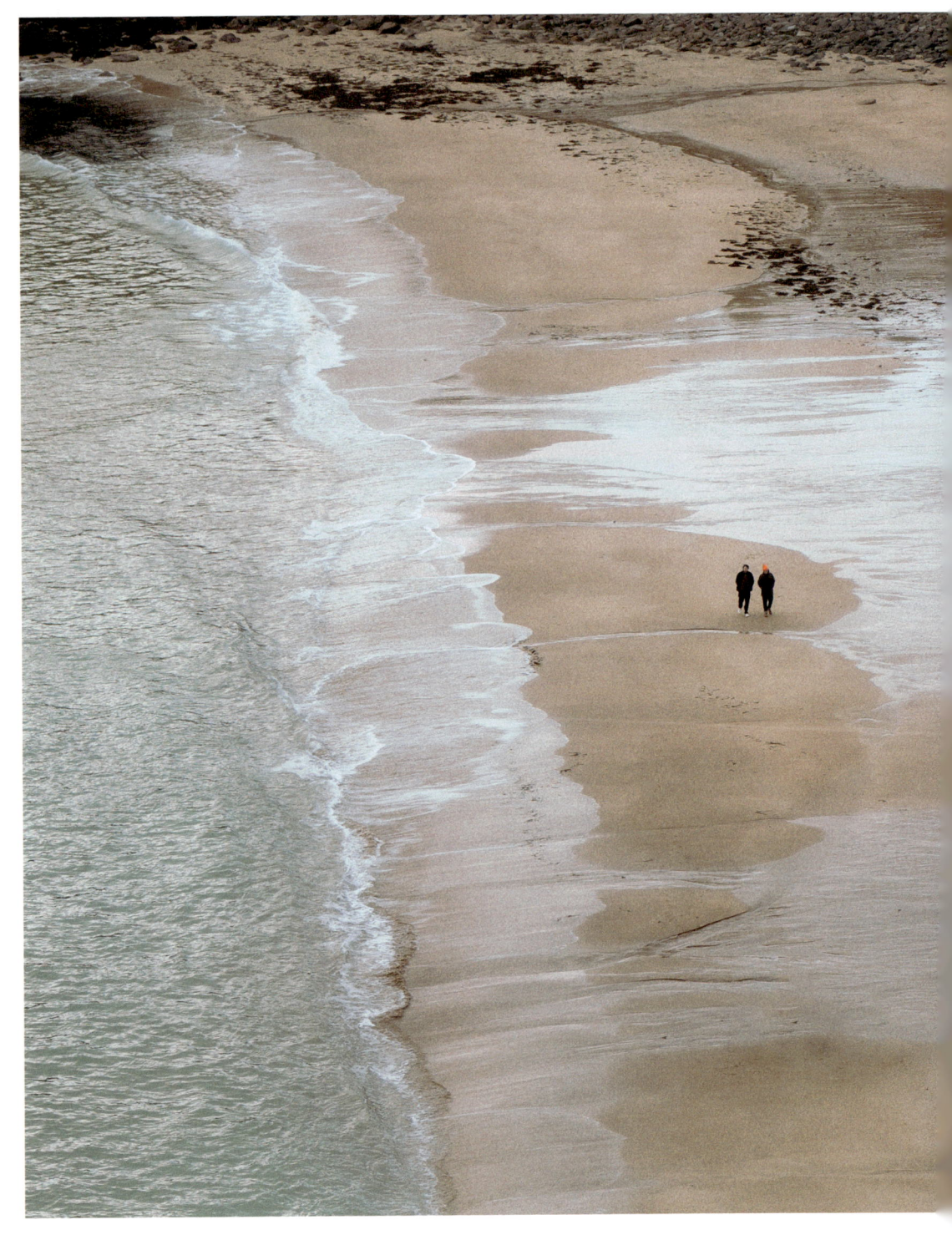

BEEN THERE, MYTHBUSTED THAT

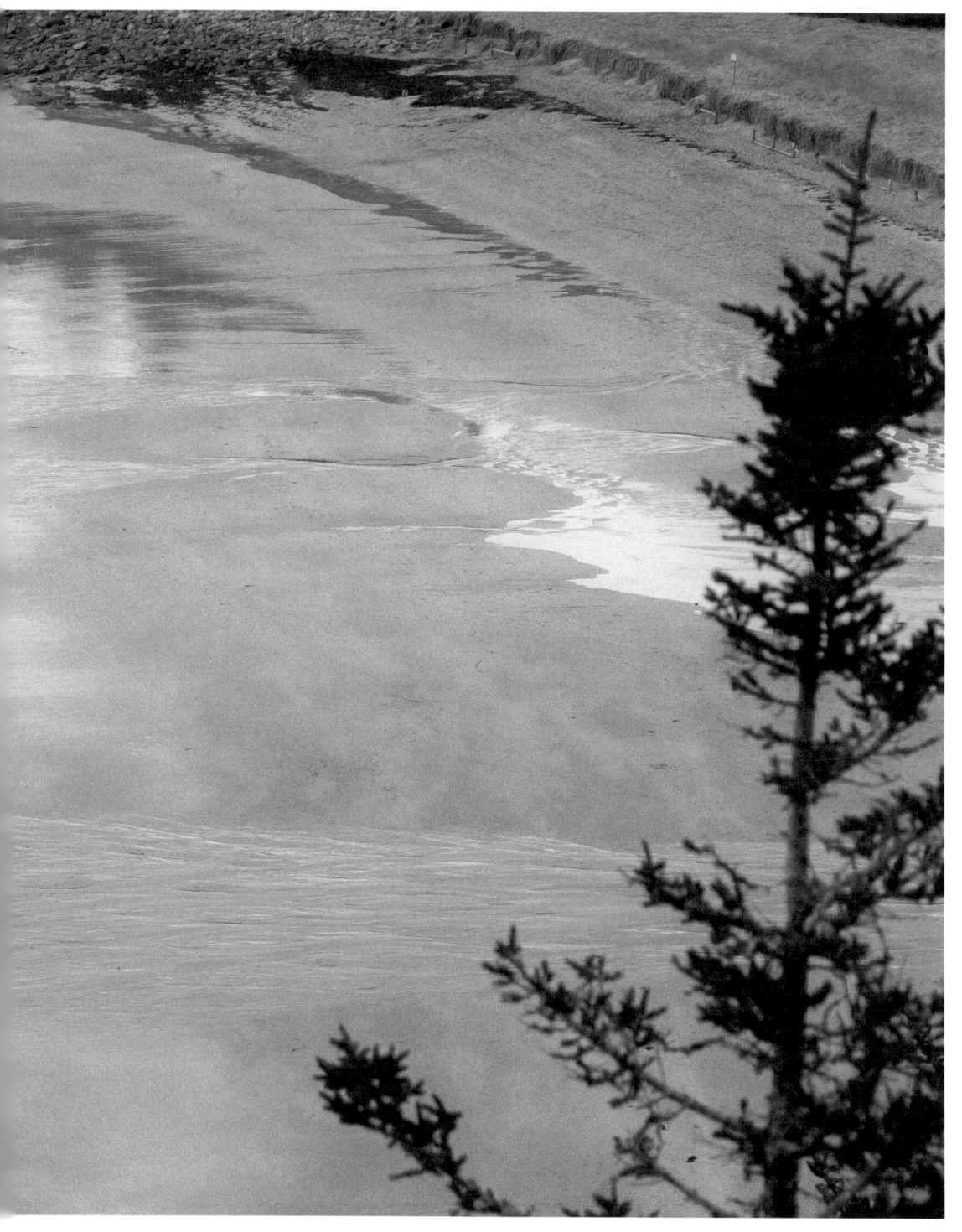

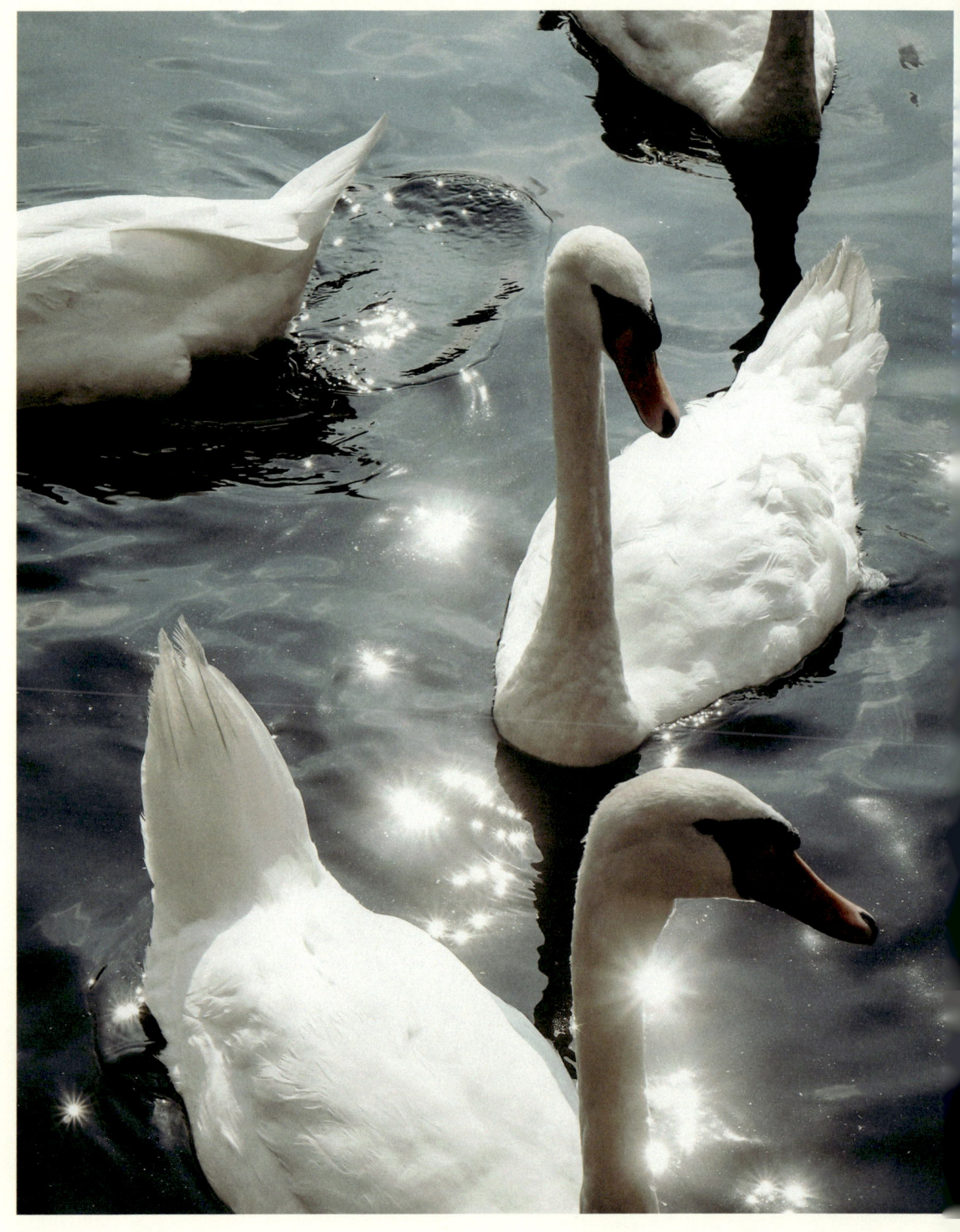

BEEN THERE, MYTHBUSTED THAT

Myth

CONTROL YOUR DESTINY

Truth
A LIFE OF NO REGRETS

1995, Yosemite National Park. I was camping with my college roommates in the wilderness, and a forest ranger's urgent call bore unforeseen news. My father, thousands of miles away in Hong Kong, had undergone emergency surgery that was ultimately unsuccessful, heralding the dawn of a new chapter.

Fast forward to 1996, where the stage shifted to the grandeur of the Atlanta Olympics. Amidst this whirlwind of events, life veered into somber territory. My mother's stroke, a cruel twist of fate, thrust my family into a tumultuous sea of uncertainty. As she succumbed to her battle, cancer silently took root within her body, leading to her departure five months later.

These raw and tangible experiences marked deep transformations, amplifying the fragility of life and kindling introspection. This voyage was not limited to sorrow; instead, it forged an unwavering commitment to live without remorse. My wife, Maryann, and I realized that the promise of tomorrow is not guaranteed, and every single moment demands to be lived to its zenith, glorifying the divine presence.

Amid these contemplations, I return to the wisdom of Matthew 6:34: "Therefore, do not worry about tomorrow, for tomorrow will worry about itself. Each day has enough trouble of its own." This verse resonates, serving as a poignant reminder to anchor ourselves in the present.

Thus began our journey, embarking on a quest for a life unburdened by regrets. The stark understanding that tomorrow's course remains elusive fortified our resolve. We relinquished the practice of saving experiences for an uncertain future, choosing instead to seize every day as a gift and a tribute to God's glory.

The echo of Matthew 13:42 serves as a cautionary tale: "And will throw them into the blazing furnace, where there will be weeping and gnashing of teeth." This image of eternal regret fueled our pursuit of a life lived to the fullest, free from the shackles of remorse.

Losing my parents at ages thirty-eight and forty-one illuminated life's fragility and its potential abrupt end. A cursory glance at the newspaper reveals the multitude of unforeseen deaths that transpire. Surely, you have encountered the abrupt and jarring news of loved ones passing away. My mother was a planner; she meticulously outlined the experiences she hoped to embrace in her later years, particularly with her grandchildren. Yet, many of these aspirations remained unfulfilled due to her untimely departure.

In 2004, another unforeseen twist emerged. My wife, Maryann, faced a cancer diagnosis. The echoes of her worries mirrored our past, yet this time a profound realization brought solace. As we navigated this trial, our faith anchored us, and the fear of death was replaced by an understanding that it is merely a transition to eternal life. Maryann was concerned about the care of our children if she would die. But when I asked her to confirm whether she had any regrets after our lifestyle change in 2000, her answer was a resounding no. Our commitment to live a life of no regrets prepared us for the worst-case scenario. She then felt calmed, and her incredible recovery was a testimony and blessing that we are eternally grateful for.

This transformative journey extended to our daughter, Tracy, who joined our company during Maryann's challenge. Her presence, instrumental in propelling our business's growth, emerged as an unforeseen gift amid turmoil.

But the story didn't culminate there. In 2007, Tracy was diagnosed with unyielding ovarian cancer. Her resilience and survival—and her continued resolution for a life of no regrets—bore witness to the enduring power of faith and grace. This tale of personal transformation underscores God's orchestration of events in our lives. The lessons learned serve as reminders of a divine blueprint that transcends our own desires.

Choosing a life of no regrets is choosing surrender. Galatians 2:20 encapsulates this essence: "I have been crucified

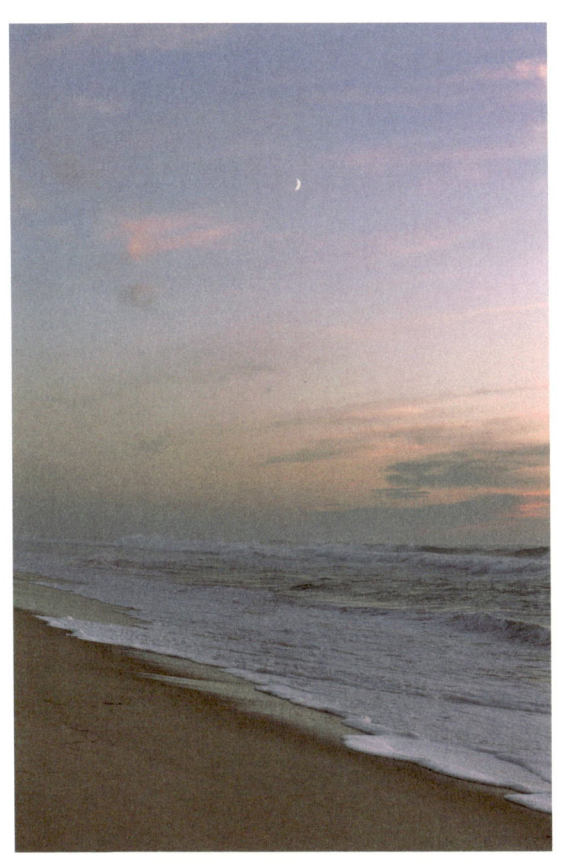

with Christ, and I no longer live, but Christ lives in me." This complete submission reshapes our lives, steering us away from worldly patterns of needing control. It is a whole life of surrender—even persecution. A life that transforms us to live completely unburdened by regrets, woven within the grand tapestry of God's greater plan.

The doctrine of living a life without regrets finds its roots deep within my theological understanding of hell. Many evangelists adhere to a transactional theology that employs hell as the ultimate threat for those who don't embrace Jesus Christ, using it as the ticket to heaven. I have always found the imagery of eternal burning in hell perplexing. If we can endure perpetual flames, why be concerned? If fire causes pain but not death, and we are already deceased, why fret over chronic pain? Don't many people experience such pain during earthly existence?

Specific Bible verses are unsettling:

- Psalm 112:10: *"The wicked will see it and be vexed, He will gnash his teeth and melt away; the desire of the wicked will perish."*
- Luke 13:28: *"In that place there will be weeping and gnashing of teeth when you see Abraham and Isaac and Jacob and all the prophets in the kingdom of God, but yourselves being thrown out."*
- Matthew 8:12: *"But the sons of the kingdom will be cast out into the outer darkness; in that place there will be weeping and gnashing of teeth."*
- Matthew 13:42: *"And will throw them into the furnace of fire; in that place there will be weeping and gnashing of teeth."*
- Matthew 22:13: *"Then the king said to the servants, 'Bind him hand and foot, and throw him into the outer darkness; in that place there will be weeping and gnashing of teeth.'"*
- Matthew 24:51: *"And will cut him in pieces and assign him a place with the hypocrites; in that place there will be weeping and gnashing of teeth."*
- Matthew 25:30: *"Throw out the worthless slave into the outer darkness; in that place there will be weeping and gnashing of teeth."*

These verses vividly illustrate what eternal regret might feel like—a ceaseless state of weeping and gnashing of teeth. Can you remember the last time you felt the wrenching emotion of regret? Hence, if you choose, hell could be an existence marked by perpetual regret—a continuous review of your life from start to finish. Throughout this contemplation, you would realize how God extended invitations to you throughout your life, which you repeatedly ignored. Reading this book is yet another invitation.

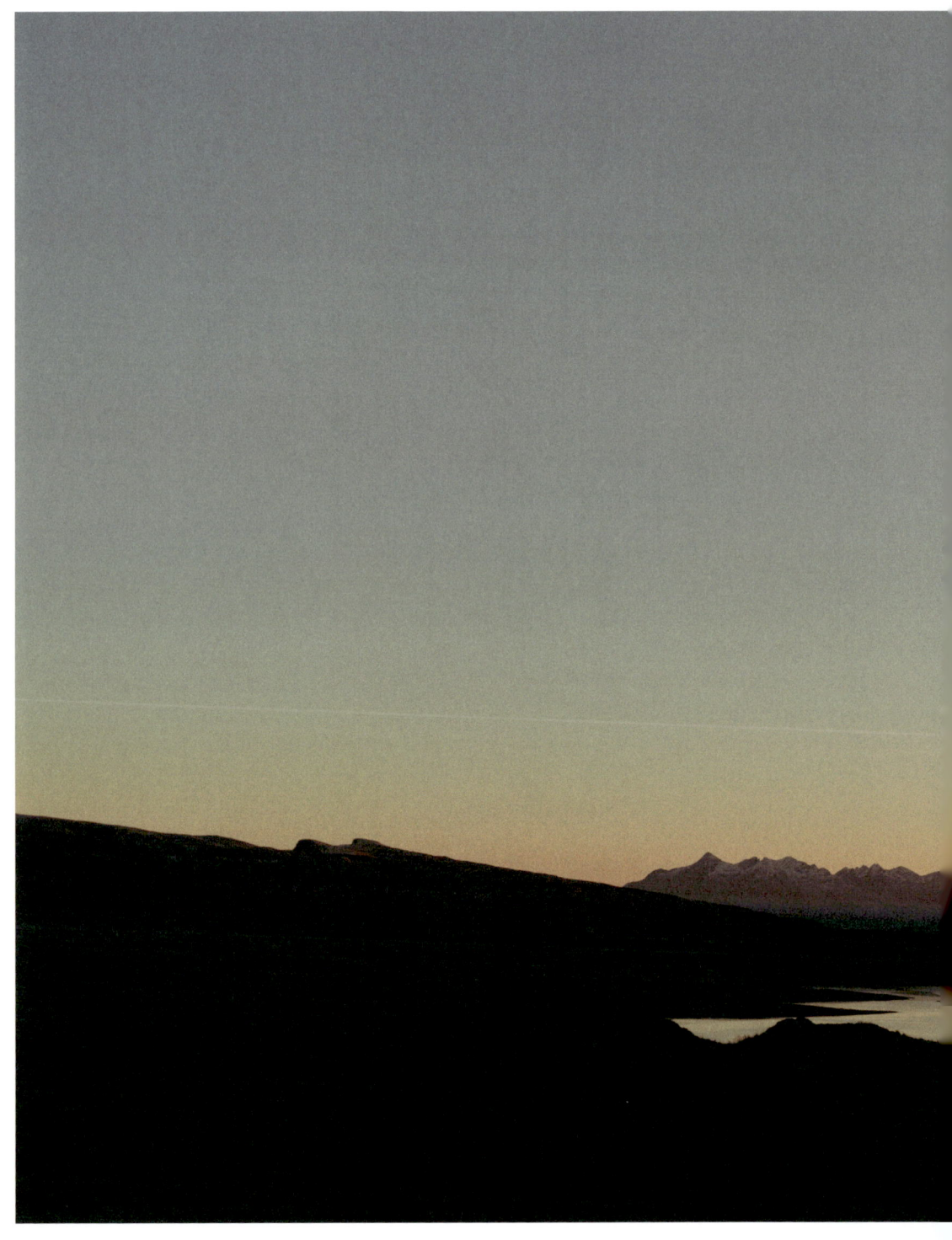

BEEN THERE, MYTHBUSTED THAT

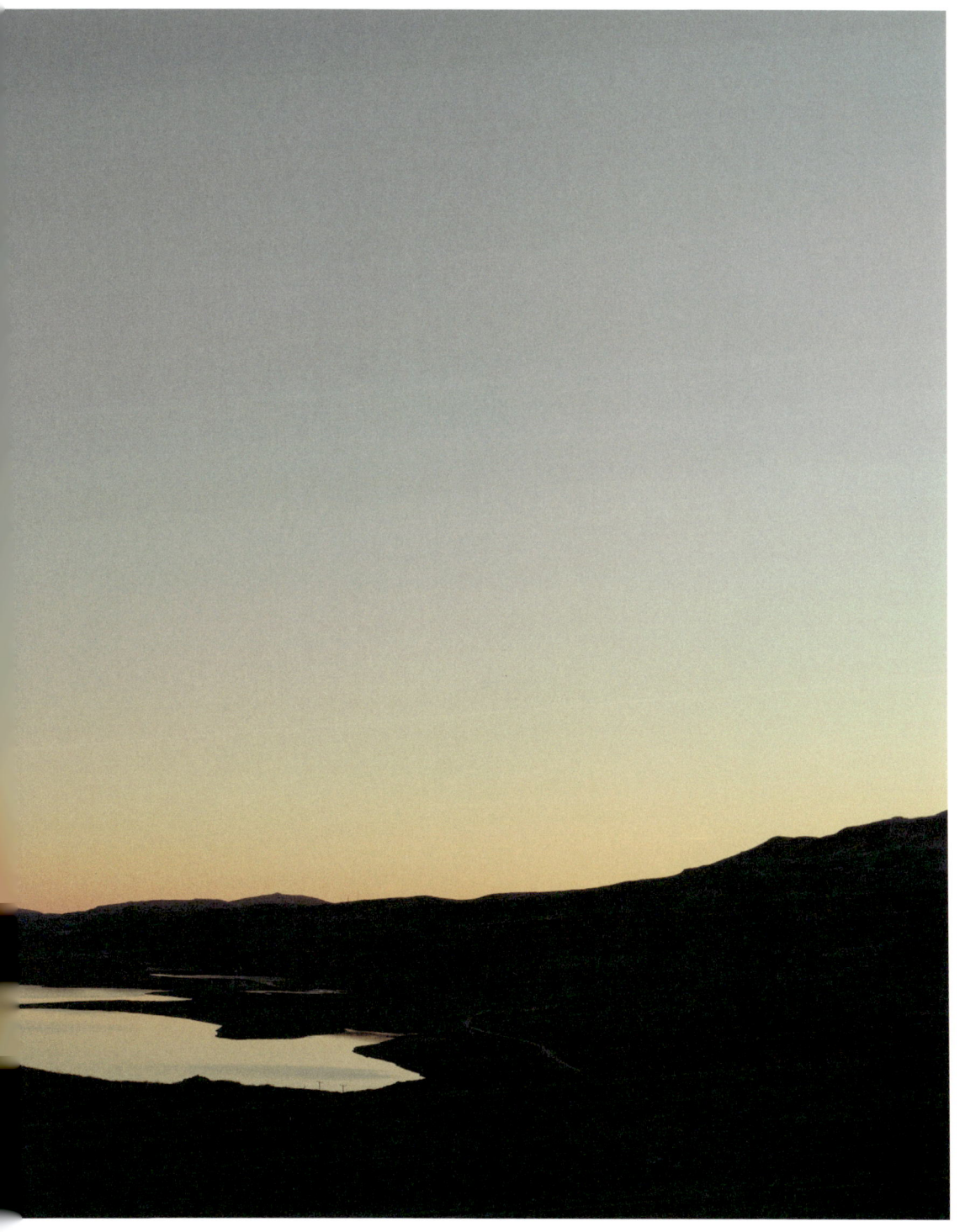

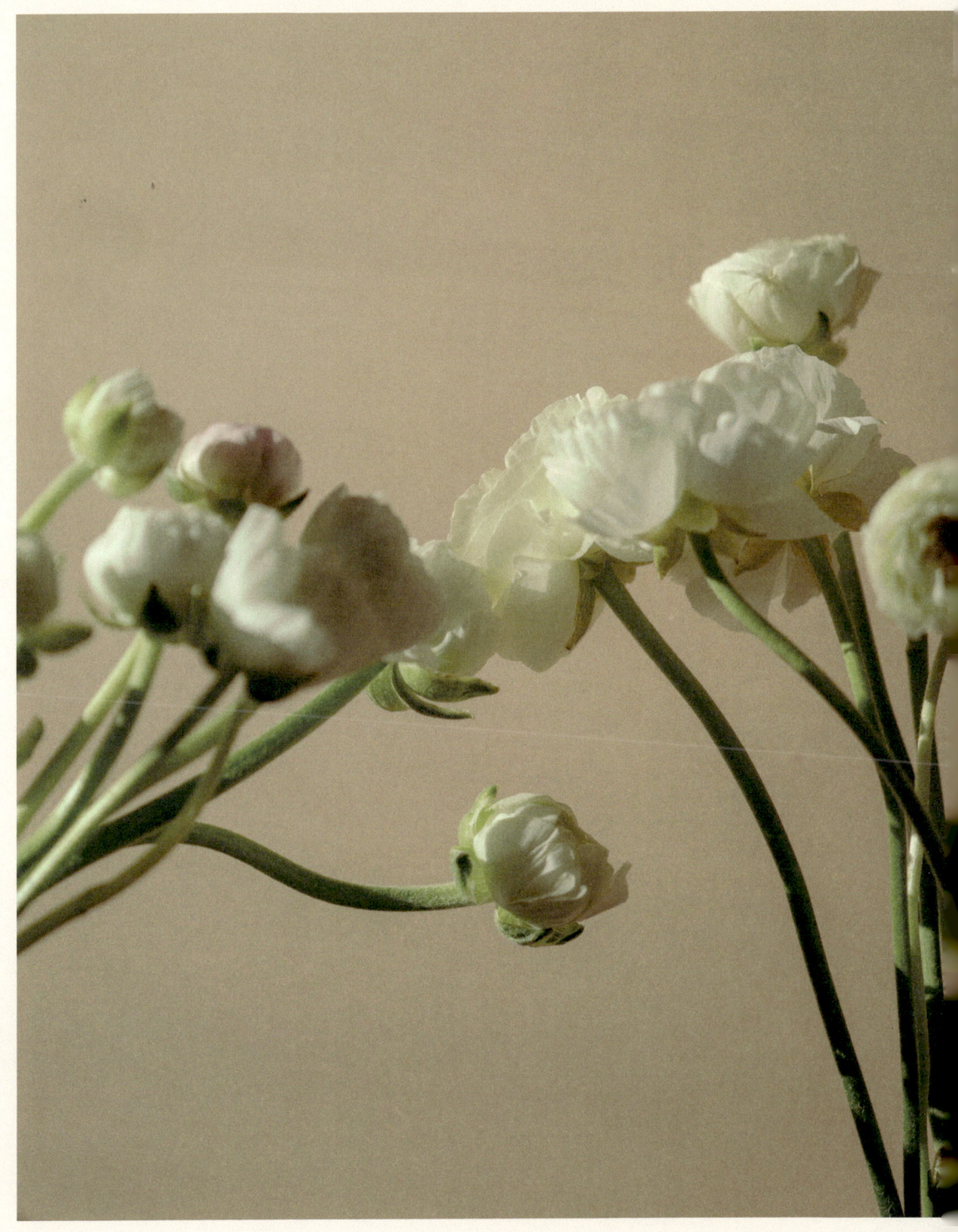

BEEN THERE, MYTHBUSTED THAT

Myth

AS A GOOD PERSON, I DESERVE A GOOD LIFE

Truth
THE BASELINE OF LIFE IS SUFFERING

In my mentorship encounters, a crucial foundation we lay is redefining life's baseline. Many, especially people of faith, cling to the notion that if I am "good" then life should yield a smooth path. Yet the reality is that life is rife with challenges, injustices, sicknesses, and disappointments. From minor inconveniences to deep tribulations, our journey is colored by adversity, and the baseline of life is suffering.

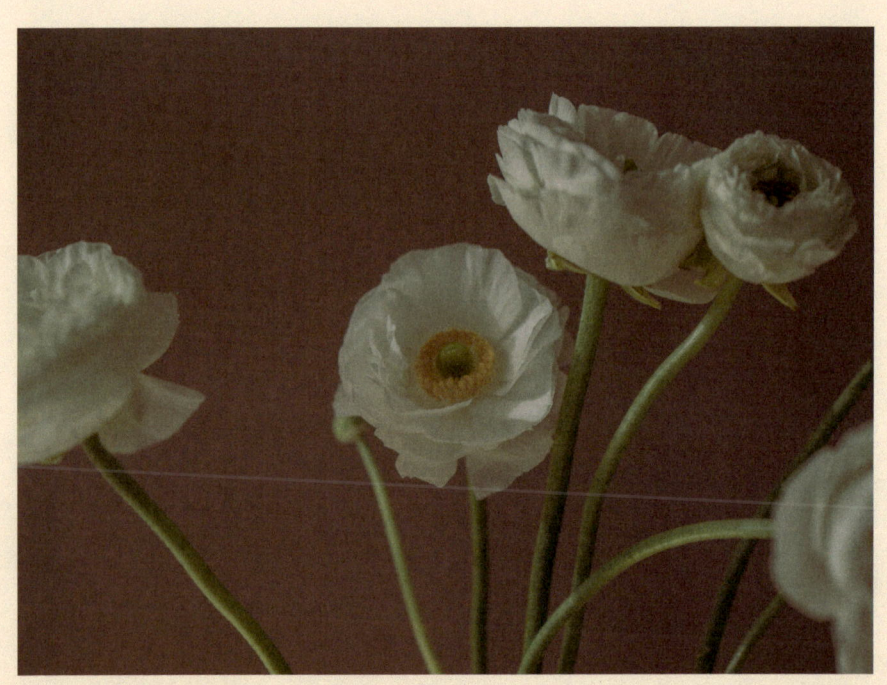

BEEN THERE, MYTHBUSTED THAT

When we face the truth of this reality we have two choices. The first is to spiral into nihilism, cynicism, and despair. The second is to persevere through suffering, finding goodness amidst pain and embracing the paradox that God is unveiled in the midst of adversity. I encourage the latter path.

Romans 5:3-4 imparts profound wisdom: "Not only so, but we also glory in our sufferings, because we know that suffering produces perseverance; perseverance, character; and character, hope." This passage underscores that suffering—or thlipsis in original Greek—serves as a catalyst for growth. When we suffer, we grow. This is what it means to be human, from the very moment we are born.

We can also consider Romans 8:28: "And we know that in all things God works for the good of those who love him, who have been called according to his purpose." God's hand orchestrates our journey, and, even in suffering, goodness dwells. God's presence fortifies us through pain, guiding our steps along the treacherous path.

Suffering does not tarnish God's faithfulness; it magnifies His love. Life is not about avoiding pain or hardships for God's promise isn't a ticket out of the world's trials. Instead, it is a pledge of divine companionship through life's trials. Embrace this paradox: suffering unveils the essence of God's love, faithfulness, and mercy. Our journey isn't invalidated by pain; it is illuminated by divine presence. Do not succumb to the misconception that God's faithfulness lies in comfort. It dwells in His constant companionship, resonating through each challenge we face.

Once we have aligned our expectations with the reality that the baseline of life is suffering, we can then freely and wholeheartedly experience gratitude when we are not experiencing pain, sickness, or any kind of suffering. Most people I know sadly miss the opportunity "to stop and smell the roses" when life does go well. In other words, do not get caught up in ephemeral inconveniences. Practice thankfulness daily and realize that we are fortunate in countless ways.

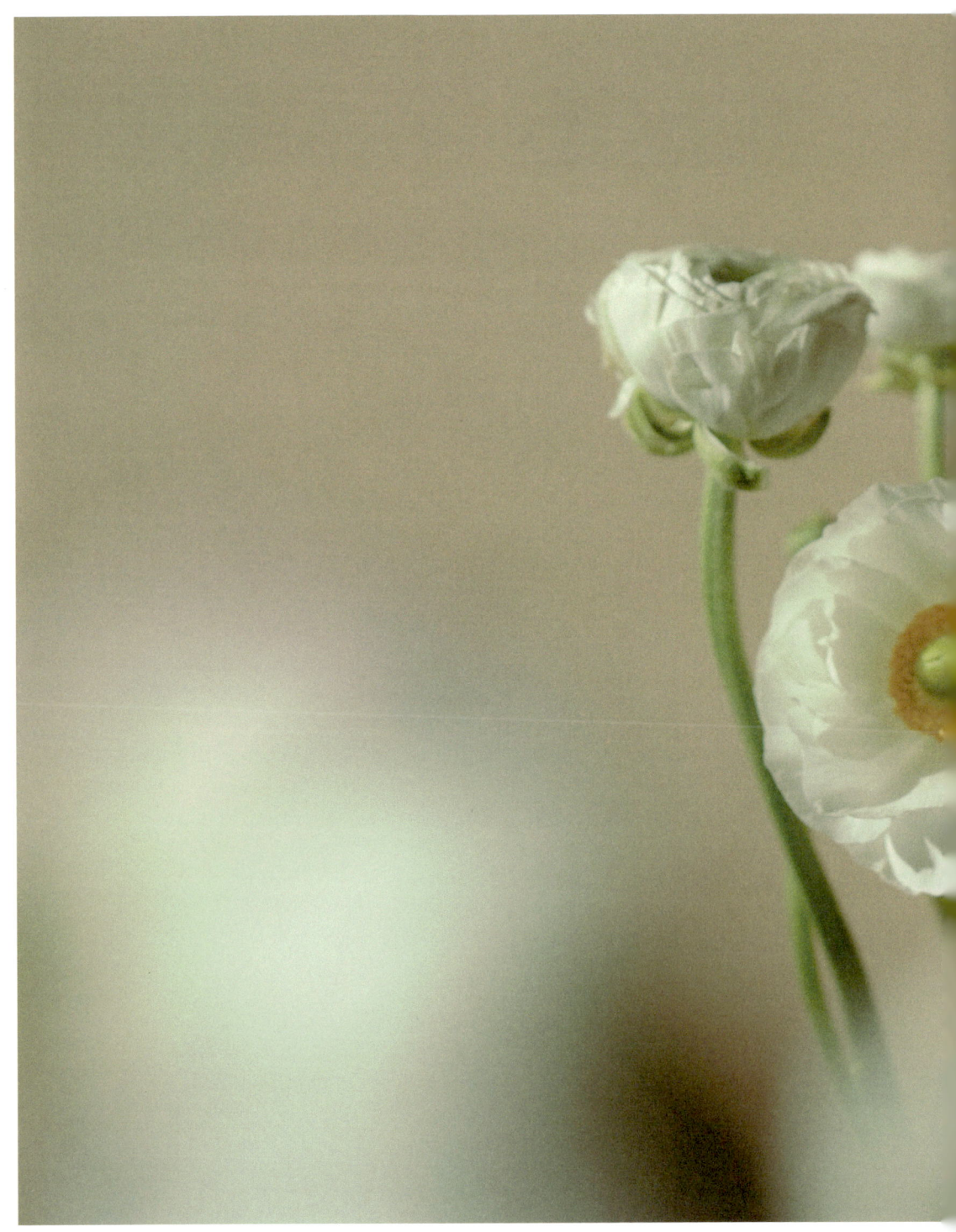

BEEN THERE, MYTHBUSTED THAT

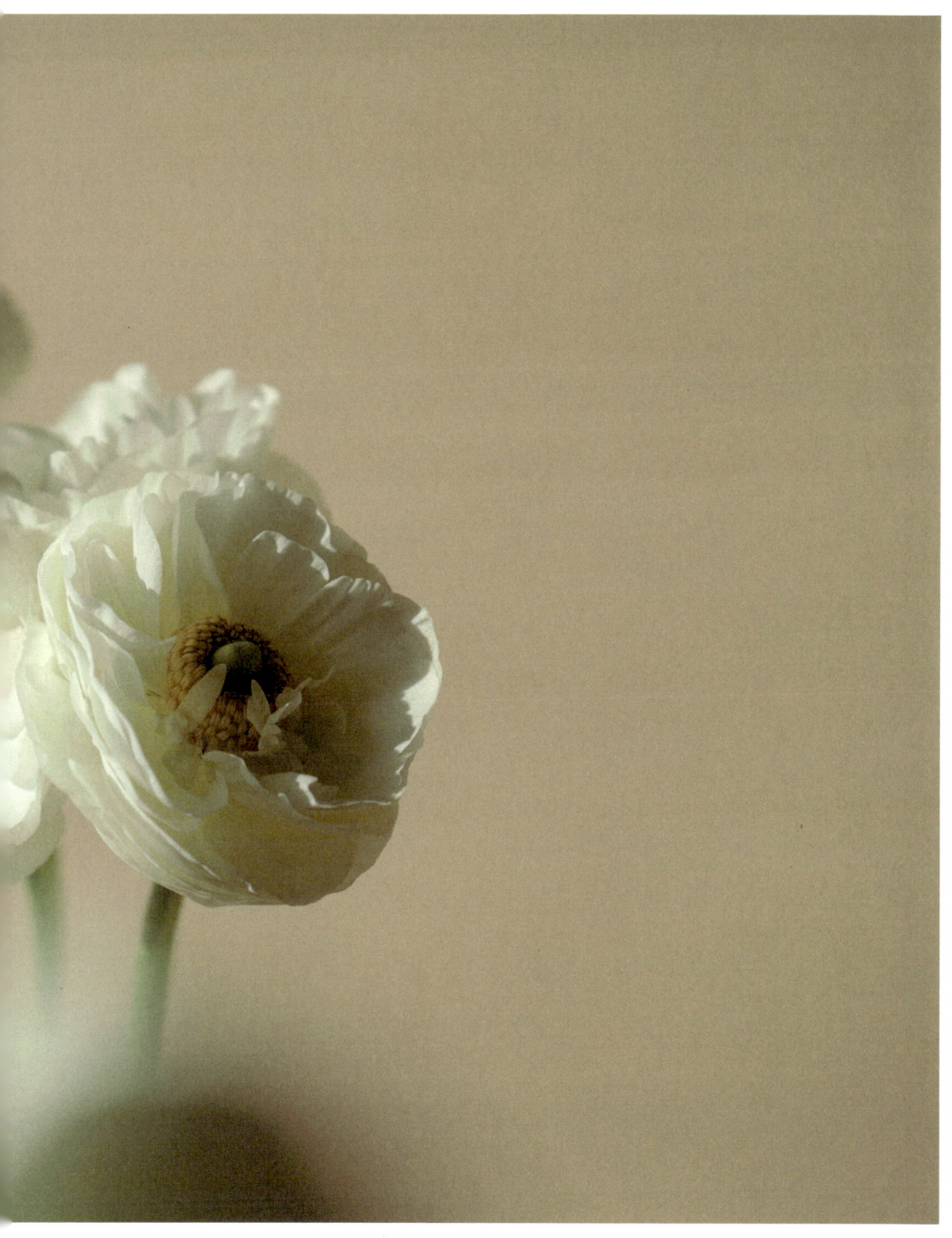

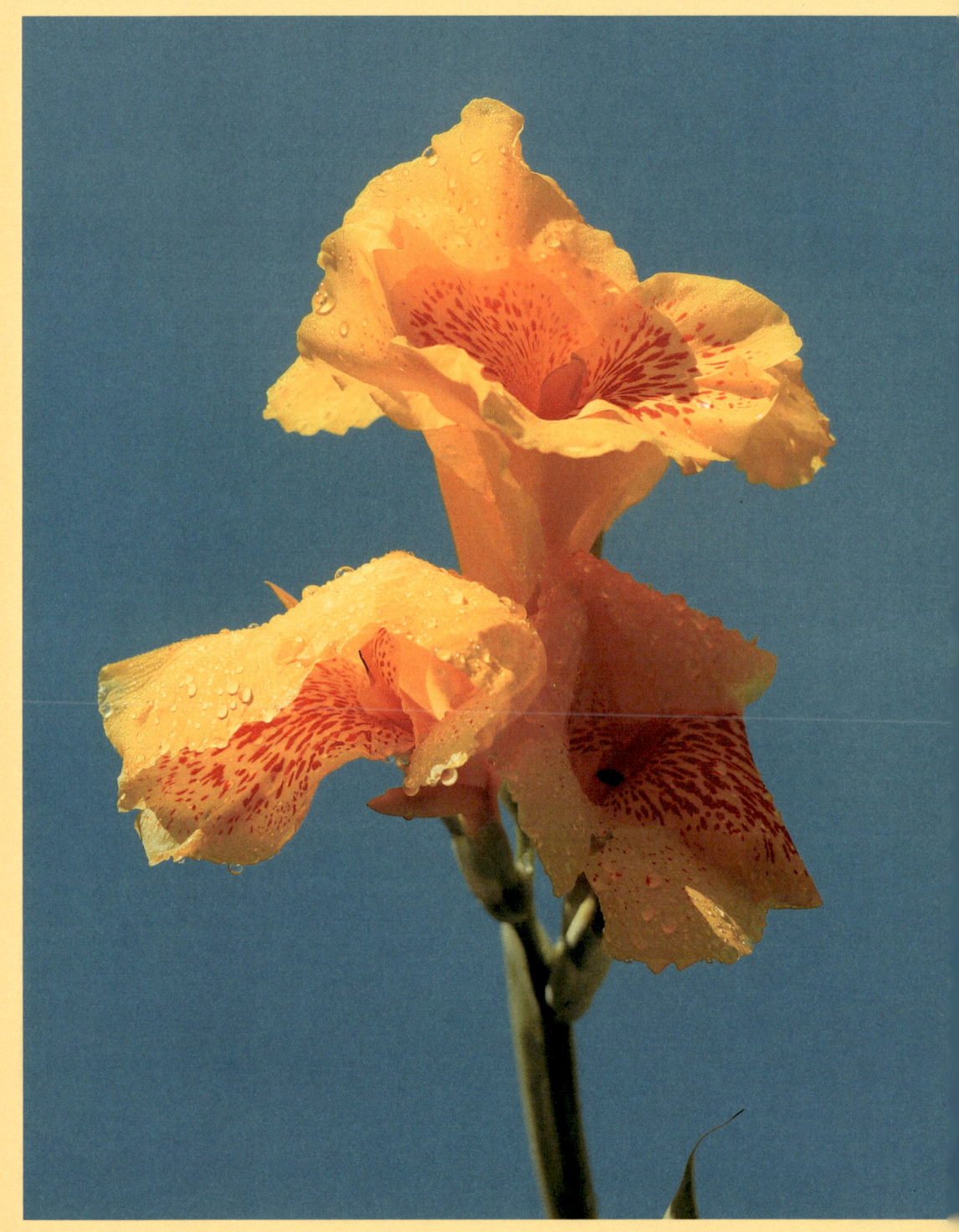

BEEN THERE, MYTHBUSTED THAT

Myth

WE LEARN IN ORDER TO BECOME MORE SUCCESSFUL

Truth
CONTINUOUS LEARNING BRINGS JOY

Imagine a newborn with the purity of innocence. As they grow, they embark on a joyful journey of learning—gaining knowledge and skills, and figuring out how to express their feelings and needs. It is a captivating adventure and a personal source of happiness as I watch my own three grandchildren grow.

For most adults, however, the simple pleasure of learning is seen as a means to an end. We only choose to "learn" when it directly leads to some form of success or advancement. This is disappointing, and the opposite of generative. Instead, we should choose continuous learning throughout our *entire* life, knowing that the process itself brings joy.

Continuous learning requires humility. There is an unseen bubble enveloping each individual, containing "what we know," "what we don't know," and "what we avoid knowing." Yet, beyond this bubble lies the infinity of "what we don't know we don't know." Grasping this reality inevitably fosters true humility—a recognition that amidst the infinite unknowns, our certainties pale. Thus, embracing a posture of genuine humility is vital.

Our perceived knowledge is not absolute truth for the expanse of the unknown dwarfs what we think we know. My personal journey has led me to an insatiable thirst for lifelong learning and its accompanying joy. From my perspective, an educated person is marked by their willingness to admit they do not know.

However, when we observe society, admitting to not knowing is akin to calling oneself foolish. Why? I discern that this lazy desire for certainty is propagated for selfish economic and political gains. The truth is always more complex than a quick comment or quip, but spreading deceit is profitable, and political motives often intertwine with financial interests, power, and ego. Radicals and idealists are manipulated by corporate interests in order to reap enormous profits. Furthermore, social media and our fast-paced lives breed short attention spans,

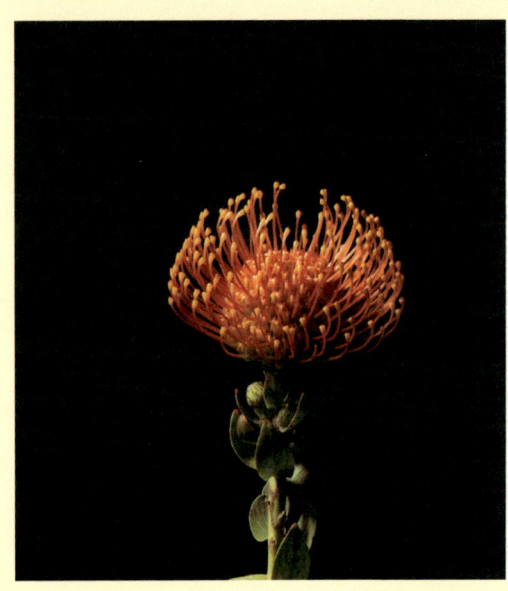

shallow thinking, the swift sharing of sensational news, and the propagation of conspiracy theories. Our motivation is garnering "likes," elevating our self-esteem. The outcome? Escalating polarization and the specter of civil unrest. This is not merely a battle between good and evil; it is a war of information. Supporters on both sides, I believe, are misled, not inherently malevolent. Labeling each other as unintelligent or insane will not mend the situation. A reset to basic education is necessary. We must ponder: what defines an educated person's behavior? How does one seek truth? How does one process and assimilate information and facts? All of these questions speak to the need for continuous learning throughout our lives. As we navigate this complex landscape, our focus must shift to cultivating true education anchored in humility, empathy, and a rigorous pursuit of knowledge.

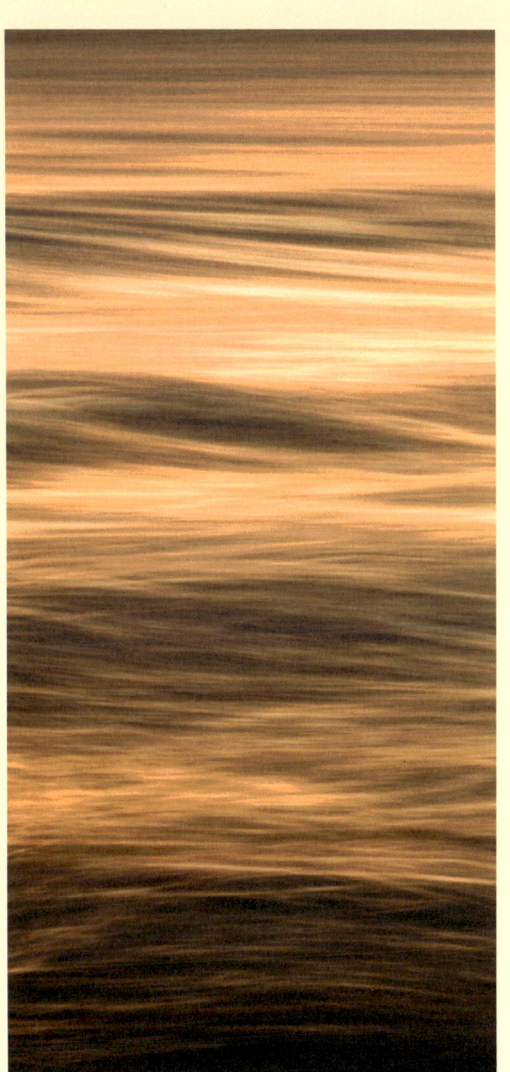

Finally, I want to share some advice on learning from my father. He said that most people have to learn from actual experience. For example, fire, even from a candle, can burn your fingers. Most people learn this by touching the flame and receiving pain. On the other hand, he said, smart and observant people learn from the experiences of others. They do not need to be burned; they pay attention to what people do around them and do not have to duplicate all of these experiences to learn.

For that reason, I strongly recommend extensive reading to my mentees. For roughly twenty dollars, we can read about an author's most significant life experiences, expressed in literature. It is an efficient way to learn from a lot of people very quickly. Imagine reading just one book a week consistently. That is fifty-two books a year, and over five hundred books in ten years.

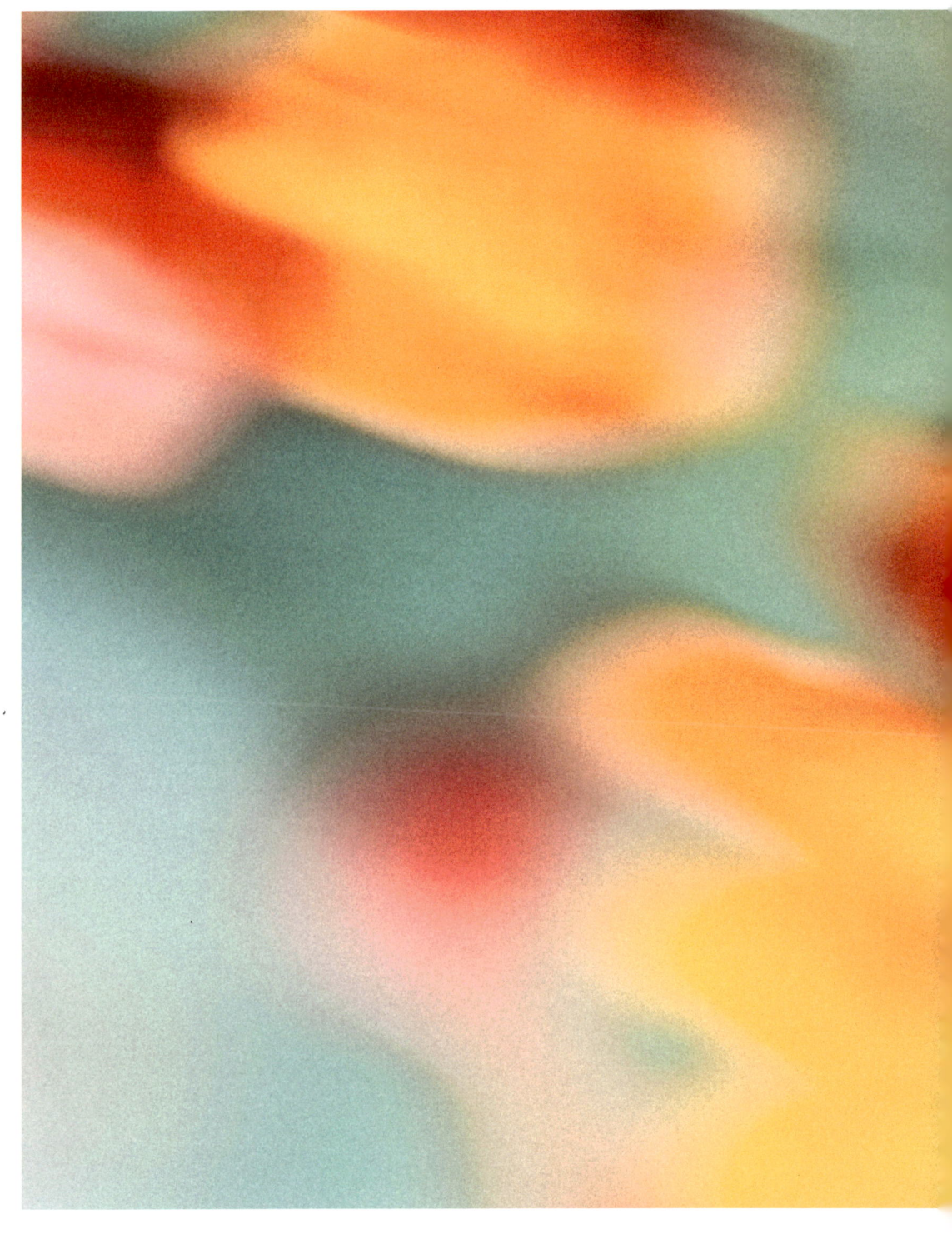

BEEN THERE, MYTHBUSTED THAT

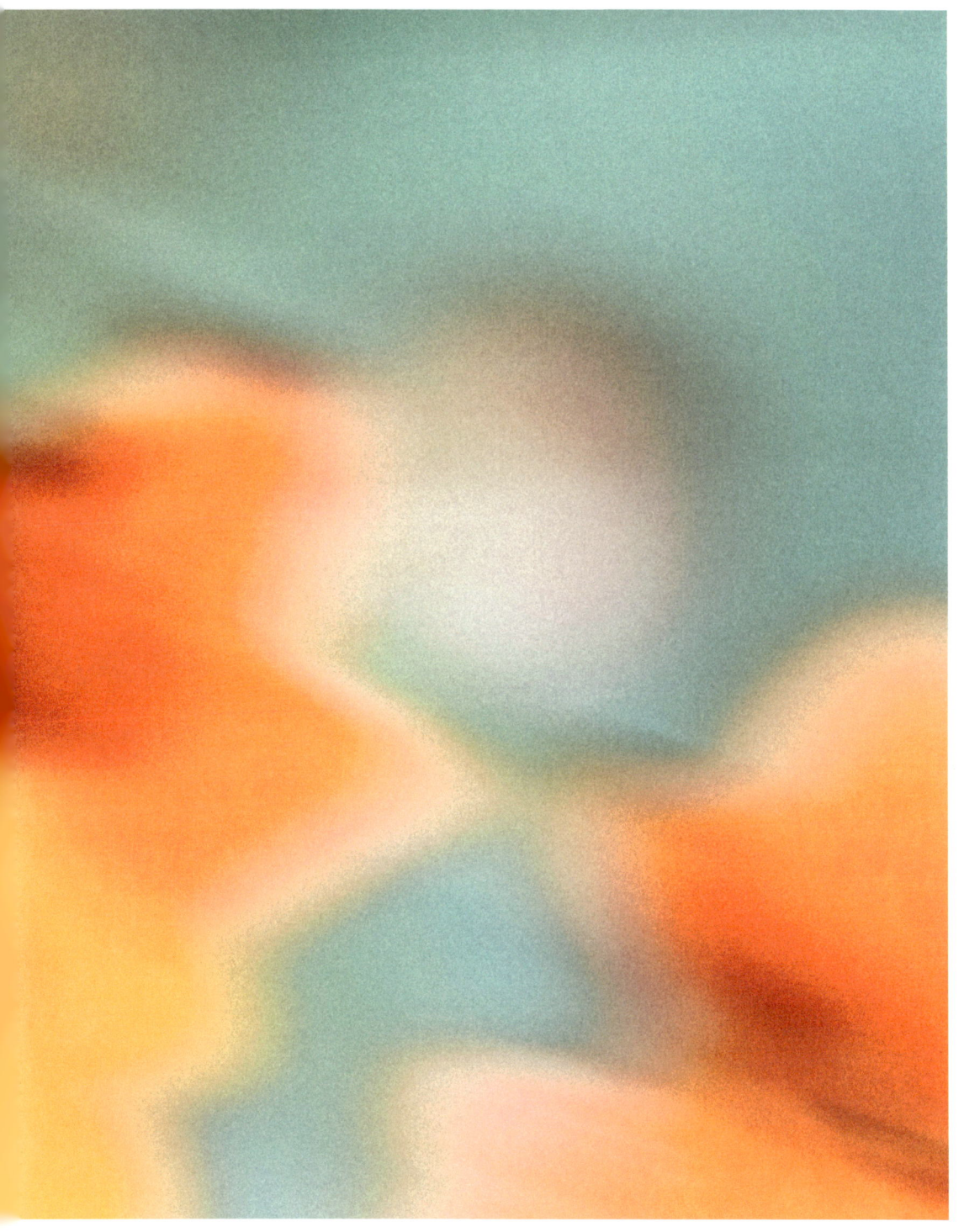

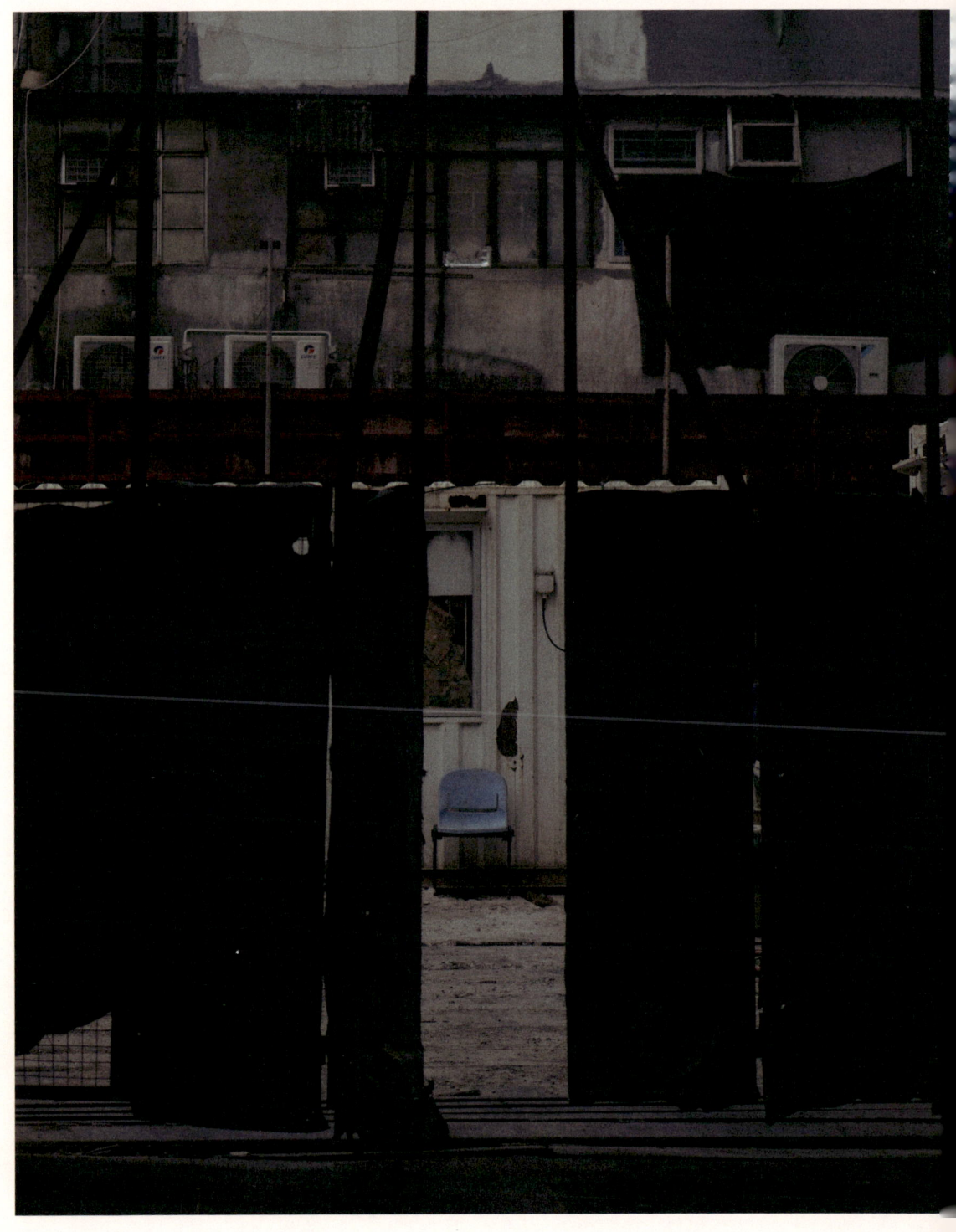

BEEN THERE, MYTHBUSTED THAT

Myth

STABILITY IS IDEAL AND PREFERRED

Truth

LIFE IS A JOURNEY OF CONSTANT CHANGE

Buddha taught that resistance to change is the root cause of pain and frustration. Our ability to embrace constant change is closely tied to our capacity for navigating the uncertainties of our future. Those who struggle with embracing change flounder at dealing with the unpredictabilities that are an inevitable part of life.

This is why I take issue with the idea of cultivating "good habits" through engaging in effective goal-setting and forming elaborate plans for the future. Inherently, these practices make us (falsely) believe we can control what is to come. But we can't—the curveballs of life are outside of our control.

Therefore, I do not advocate for long-term planning, extensive goal setting, or the rigid formation of habits. Instead, I decide my actions only after waking up each morning. I do not adhere to any set routine, checklist, or planning. I wake up whenever I choose, without an alarm, and then decide how to go about my day. I am aware this perspective arises from an immense amount of privilege—after all, we all have commitments that require our attention or timelines and boundaries that are not fully ours to decide. My intention is not to provide a step-by-step blueprint for duplication, just to challenge our culture's obsession with trying to control the future and render it stable.

From wars to natural disasters to the outbreak of deadly diseases, the future is altogether unpredictable. Every day, the news reports on events we couldn't have anticipated. Is it not a display of sheer arrogance to attempt to predict the future? Perhaps nothing has been more universally unpredictable in recent history as the COVID-19 pandemic. Initially, our company projected a significant sales decline, prompting us to reduce inventory orders and delay production. However, as time went on, we found the opposite to be true: sales were increasing! Thanks to our company's agile approach, where we focus on quarterly goals rather than long-term planning, we were able to quickly pivot back to increasing inventory. Like life, it wasn't perfect or fully smooth-sailing; however, compared to most companies' planning cycles, our short-term approach spared us wasteful spending of time and resources and allowed us to get back on track faster and stronger.

Overall, our company's culture is to start each new quarter completely anew—who we were before the pandemic is not who we were during the pandemic, and it's not who we are today. Our company embraces constant reinvention, a trait which allowed us to persevere through the pandemic with minimal losses.

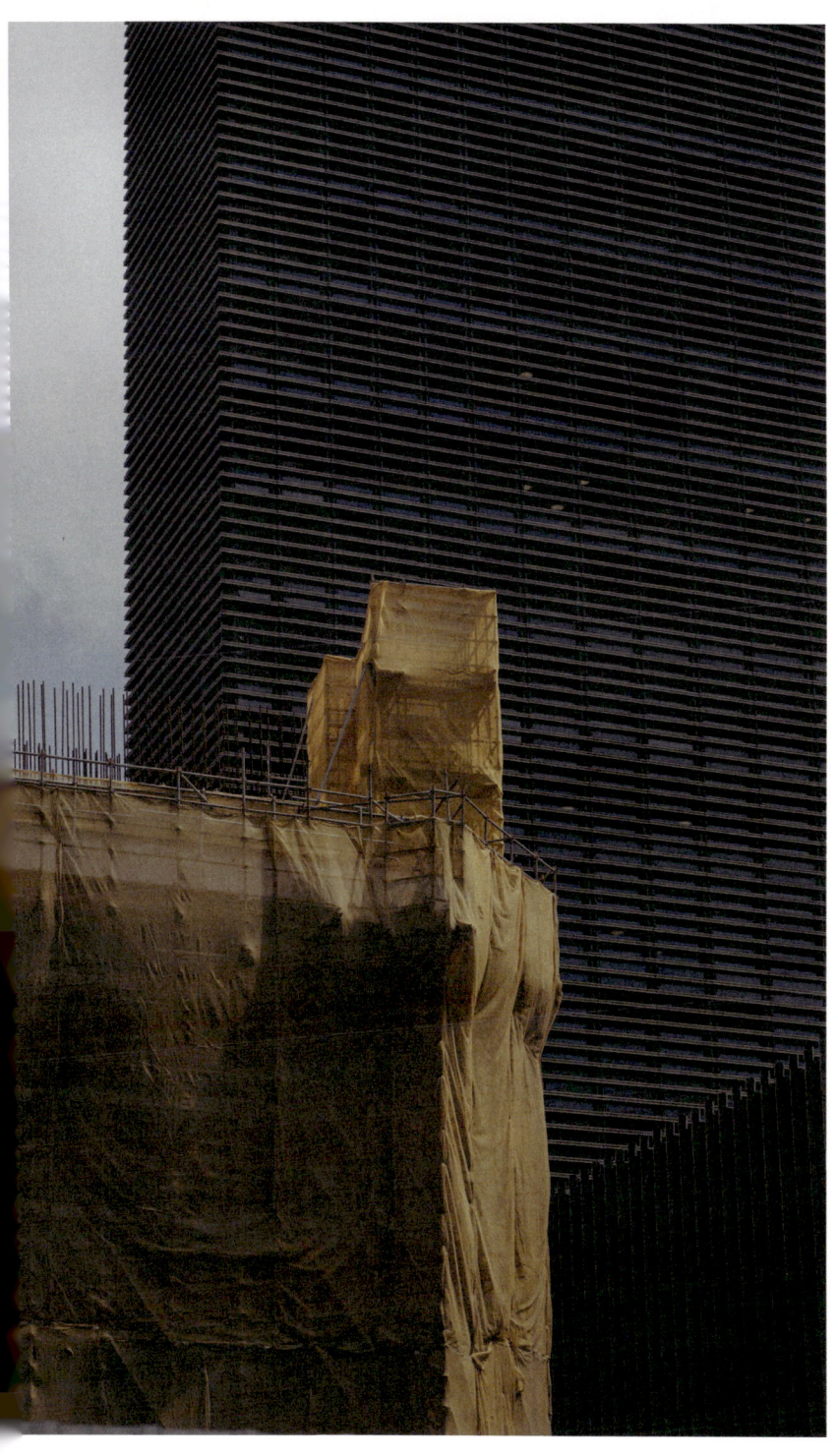

If we can all acknowledge constant change in the world and our limited knowledge of the future, then why do we invest so much time and energy in planning? Take a moment to ponder the "why" deeply. The answer might seem apparent, right? Aren't we all expected to plan? Isn't planning a fundamental skill we're taught? Isn't it a hallmark of responsibility? It is clear how planning has become an automatic choice, needing no questioning or scrutiny. It's taken for granted as a "life truth," yet it is a myth. The misconception propagated is that the more meticulously we plan, the more favorable the outcome, and the better our lives will be. But does planning deliver its promised benefits?

During my early career, I was an obsessive and diligent planner, devouring every book available on how to make my companies reach one billion dollars through a ten-year business plan. I would redo this plan over and over, trying to perfect it. Yet none of that effort yielded results! It was an utter waste of time because the world is in a state of continual change. The flaw in the underlying assumption of the planning process is that we can somehow assume a level of stability for planned events. The actuality, at best, is that a plan might pertain to a singular moment in a year. I find it astonishing how ineffective the annual plans I crafted were, and I cringe at the thought of another organization embarking on a five-year, ten-year, or even twenty-year strategic plan.

Let's take the SWOT analysis as an illustration, a fundamental component of corporate planning. In our company, our strengths (S) and weaknesses (W) are in constant flux due to our robust training programs and emphasis on ongoing learning and enhancement. Put simply, our employees are perpetually evolving, which means they address their S's and W's continuously. Thus, capturing a snapshot of SW is exactly that—a transient moment that quickly becomes outdated, philosophically and practically. Moreover, we recruit new employees throughout the year. Each additional person alters the S and W dynamics of our company. So, how could we consider snapshots as a reliable basis for our planning?

Whenever we hire a new employee, we are bringing in their résumé, meaning all their past experiences and knowledge. But we also realize that in our fast-changing world, that résumé is outdated already, unless that new employee continues to learn and improve. That is why the most important factor in our recruitment process is not how smart someone is but how good a learner they will be.

At our companies, our dedication to continuous learning and improvement is a daily commitment. We invest time and effort in our quarterly performance review meetings. These aren't labeled as quarterly *planning* meetings, nor do we engage in long-term planning sessions.

Our quarterly gatherings consist of presentations by team members, highlighting our achievements from the previous quarter, lessons learned, and areas for improvement in the upcoming quarter.

Seasons serve as nature's reminder that the world perpetually propels forward, evolving and changing. While patterns can be discerned by studying the past, what will unfold each day in the future remains a mystery. It is futile for us to endeavor to unravel this mystery with the aim of manipulating or controlling the future to our advantage. Instead, we must continuously learn how to embrace change.

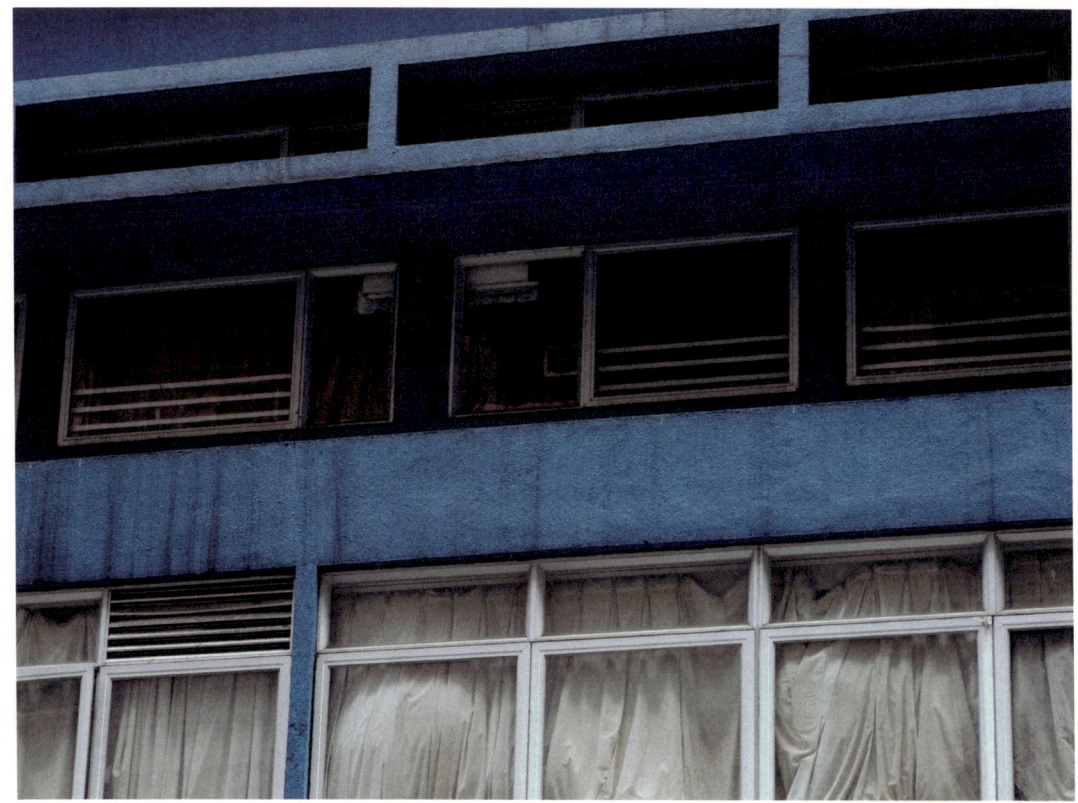

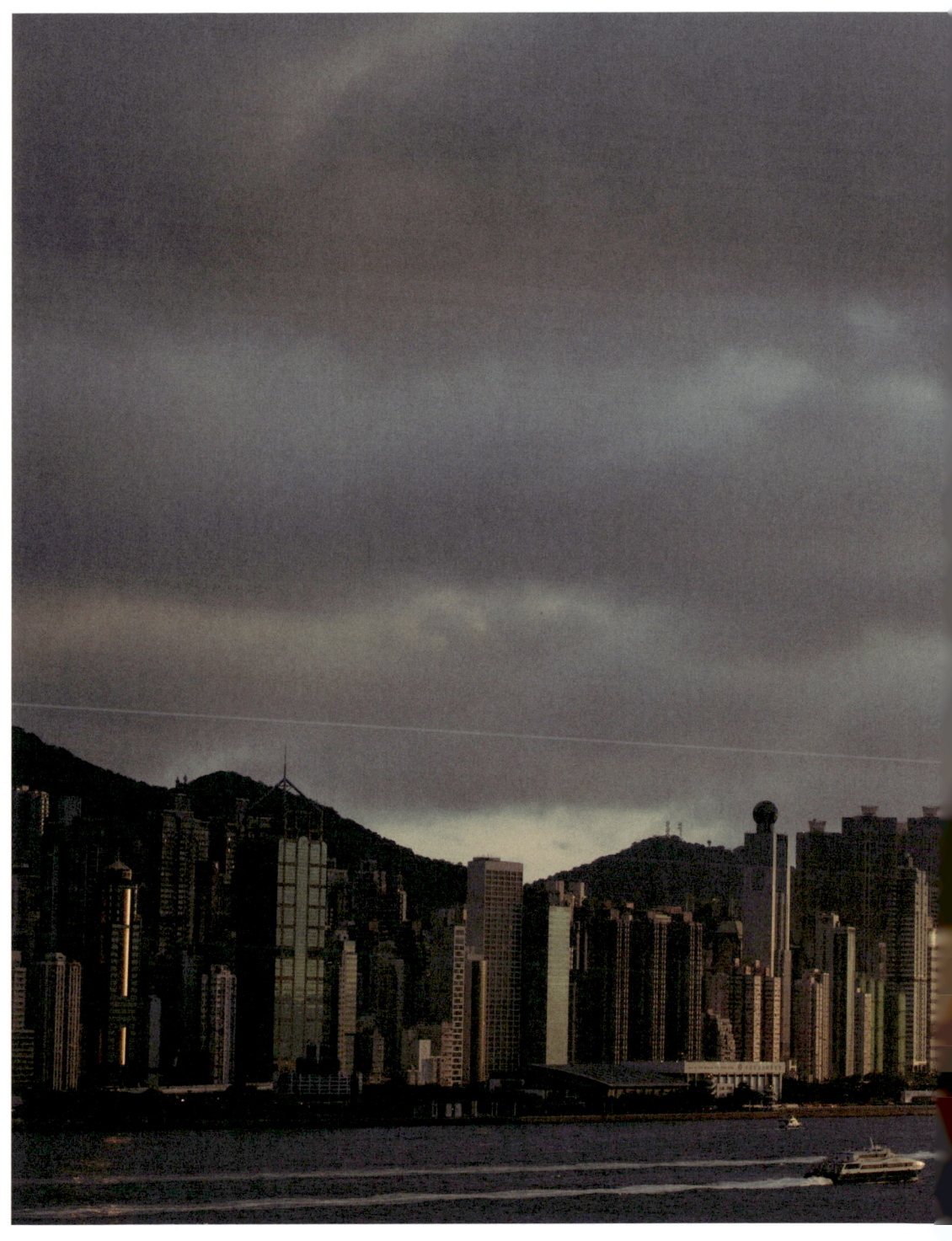

BEEN THERE, MYTHBUSTED THAT

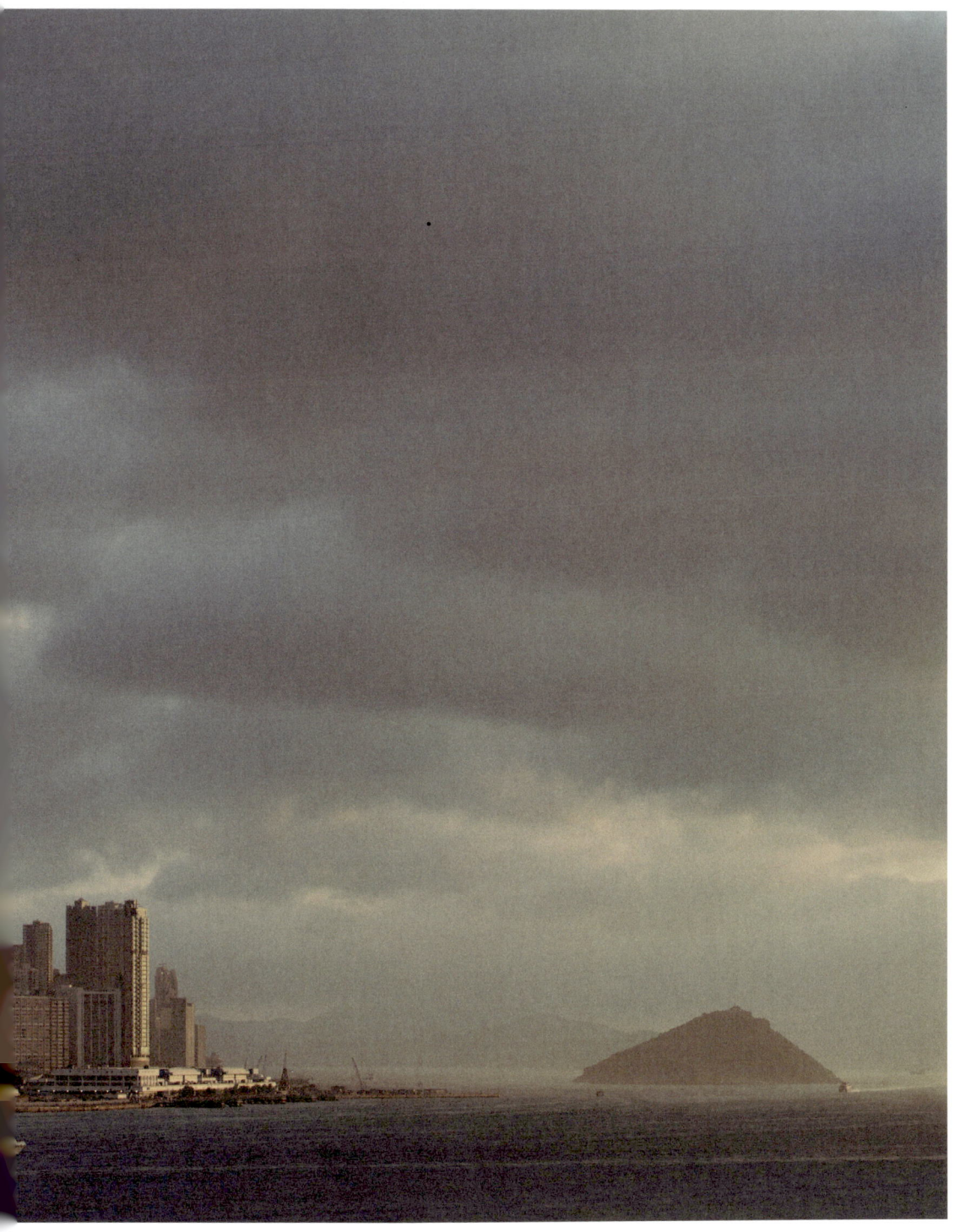

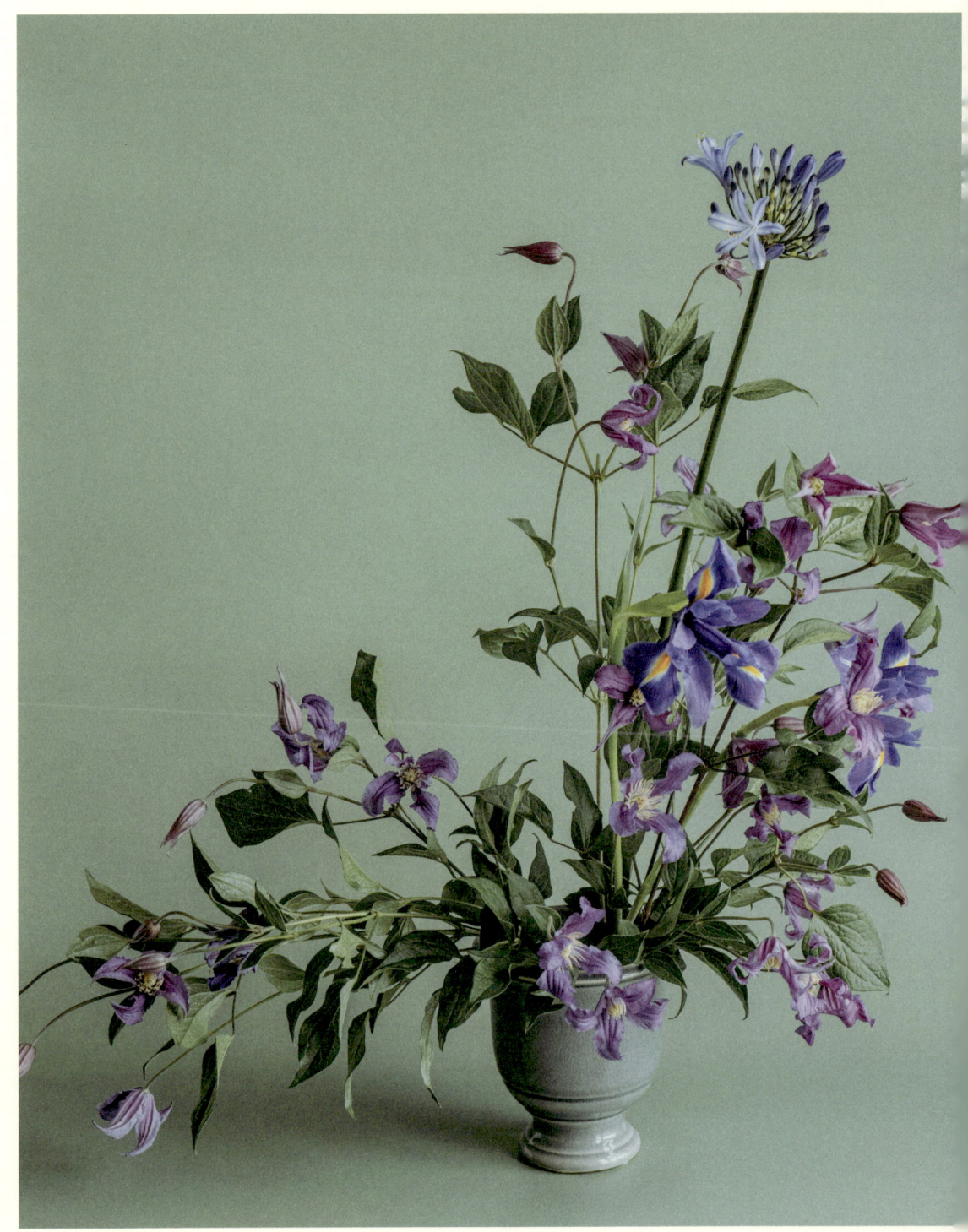

BEEN THERE, MYTHBUSTED THAT

Myth

LONG–TERM PLANNING AND BIG GOALS ARE THE BEST

Truth

DAILY EXCELLENCE MATTERS; FOCUS ON MOTIVES

In 1949, when the communists assumed control of China, my nineteen-year-old father journeyed to Hong Kong by train. He traveled with a church youth group and was assigned work at a textile factory established by a Christian entrepreneur from Shanghai. His journey marked a humble start from the very bottom, and, through unwavering dedication, he ascended the ranks.

My father's promotions hinged on a simple motto: pursue excellence in every task, every day. He regarded each assignment, even cleaning a toilet, as an opportunity to exhibit unmatched effort and intention. He approached even the lowest of tasks with the intention of outshining those who came before and after. His unique attitude earned him admiration from supervisors and peers alike, propelling him to becoming a distinguished industry manager at a remarkably young age. I can vividly recall the pride with which he recounted a time when three different factory owners vied for his employment, each attempting to entice him to join them. Amidst a wave of unemployment among his friends (due to an influx of refugees into Hong Kong) my father remained consistently employed. Not a single day of joblessness, a feat he cherished.

As a business owner, I seek employees who will continually bring excellence to their work, free from preoccupations about strategic career planning. Following my father's lead, I believe focusing on excellence alone proves sufficient. Yet, this mindset remains an uncommon trait among most individuals.

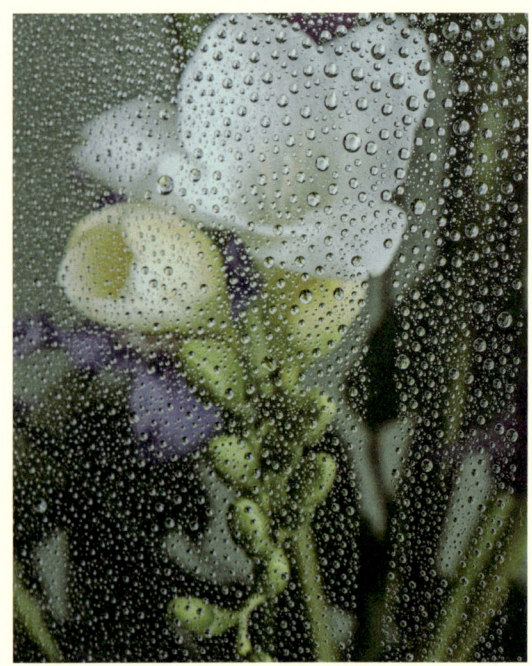

In my coaching sessions, I advocate for liberating oneself from the burden of meticulously planning and predicting a successful career and life. Instead, I encourage individuals to embrace daily presence and concentrate on embodying excellence. Rather than aiming directly for success—whatever that entails—shift your focus to cultivating excellence, and let success naturally emerge.

Guided by my father's influence, I have crafted a mantra: to manifest love for God through excellence in every endeavor and encounter. This excellence is not a mere subjective claim but an objective validation and confirmation that comes from our communities. This is an embodiment of Jesus Christ's instruction to love our neigh-

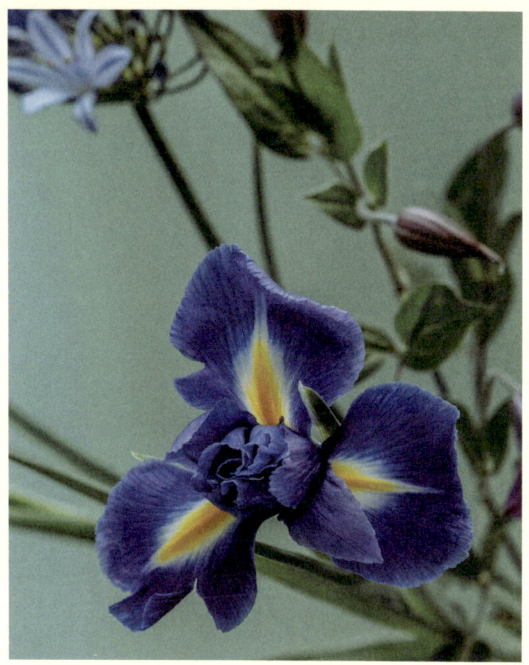

bors as ourselves. Free from anxiety about the future and the outcome of actions, I believe adhering to this mantra will consistently yield positive and loving results.

Consider the well-intentioned, but ultimately irresponsible, stereotype of many graduation speeches—when the orators preach advice like "follow your passion," "just do what you love," and the most ridiculous: "you can be whoever you want to be... just look at me." These types of aspirations are not what young graduates need to hear today. The world is a cruel place, full of suffering and injustice. Positive "dream" thinking is faulty without gaining real, solid proficiency through a commitment to daily excellence.

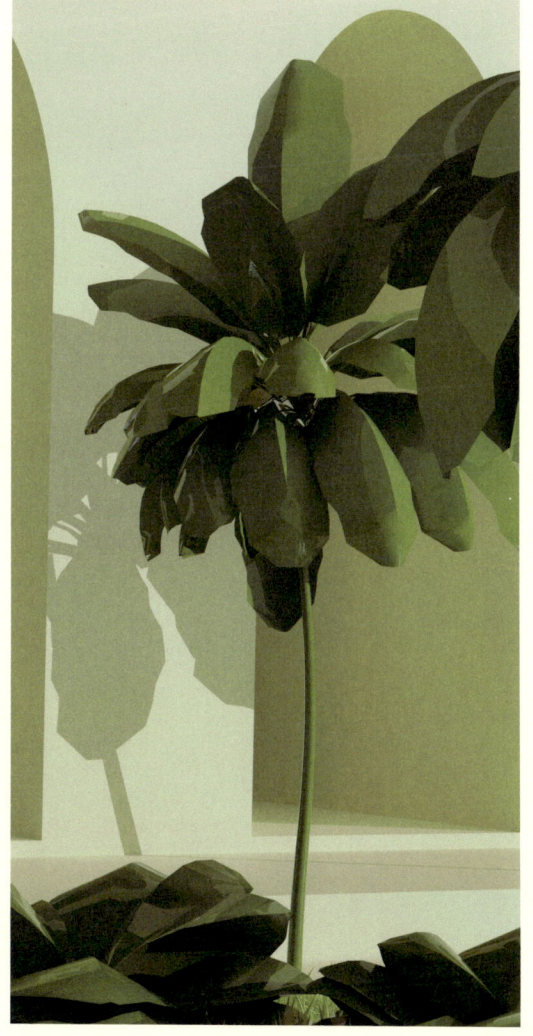

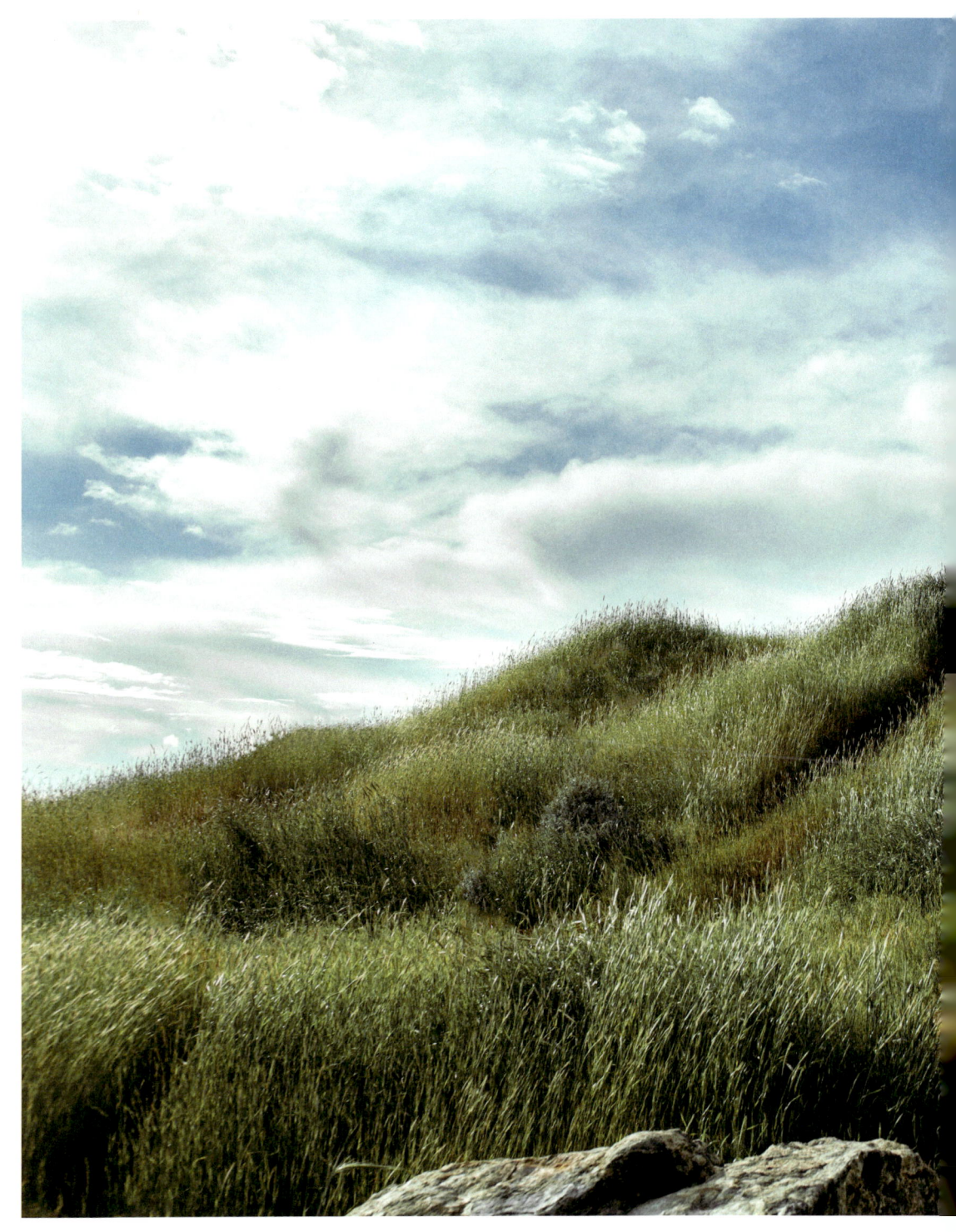

BEEN THERE, MYTHBUSTED THAT

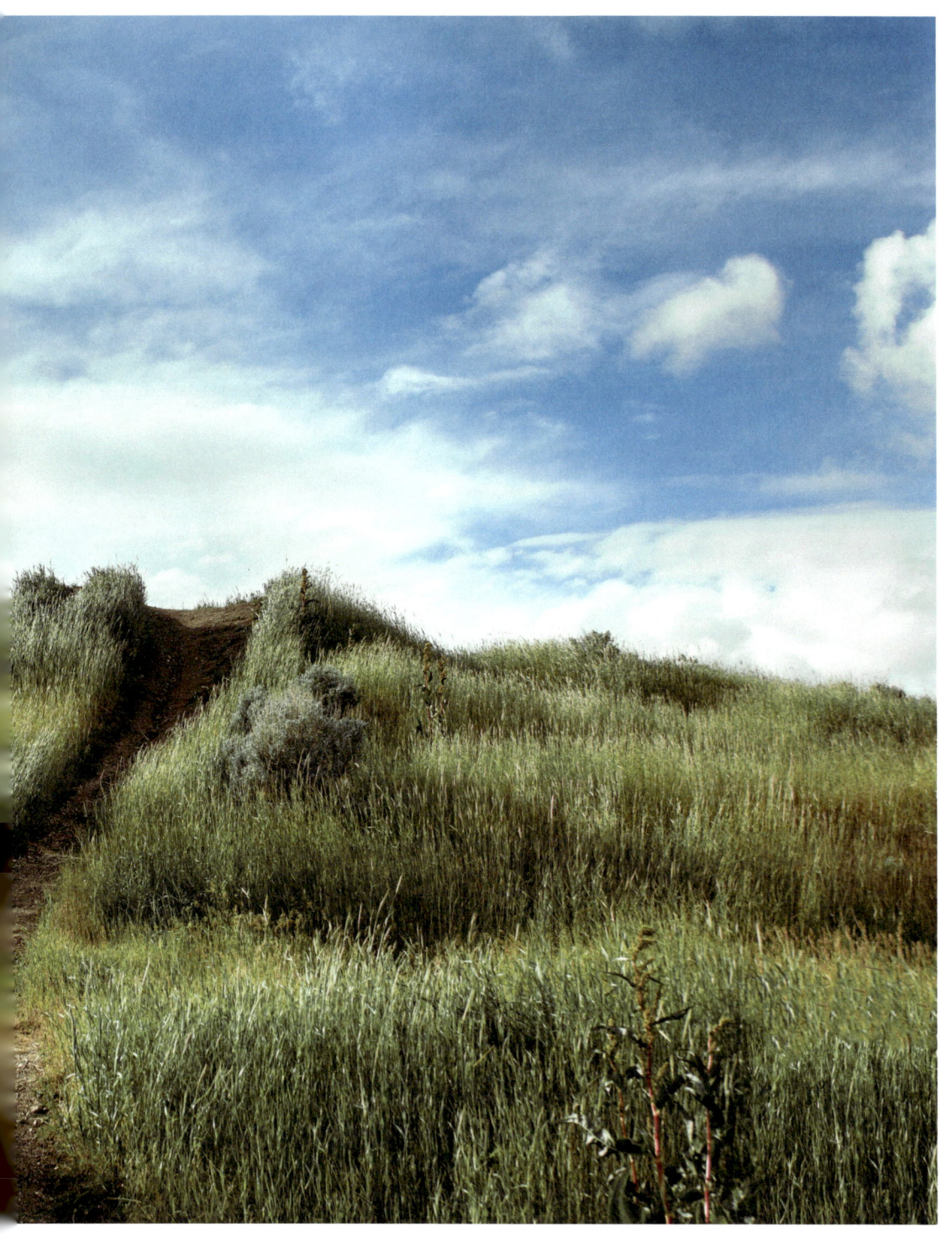

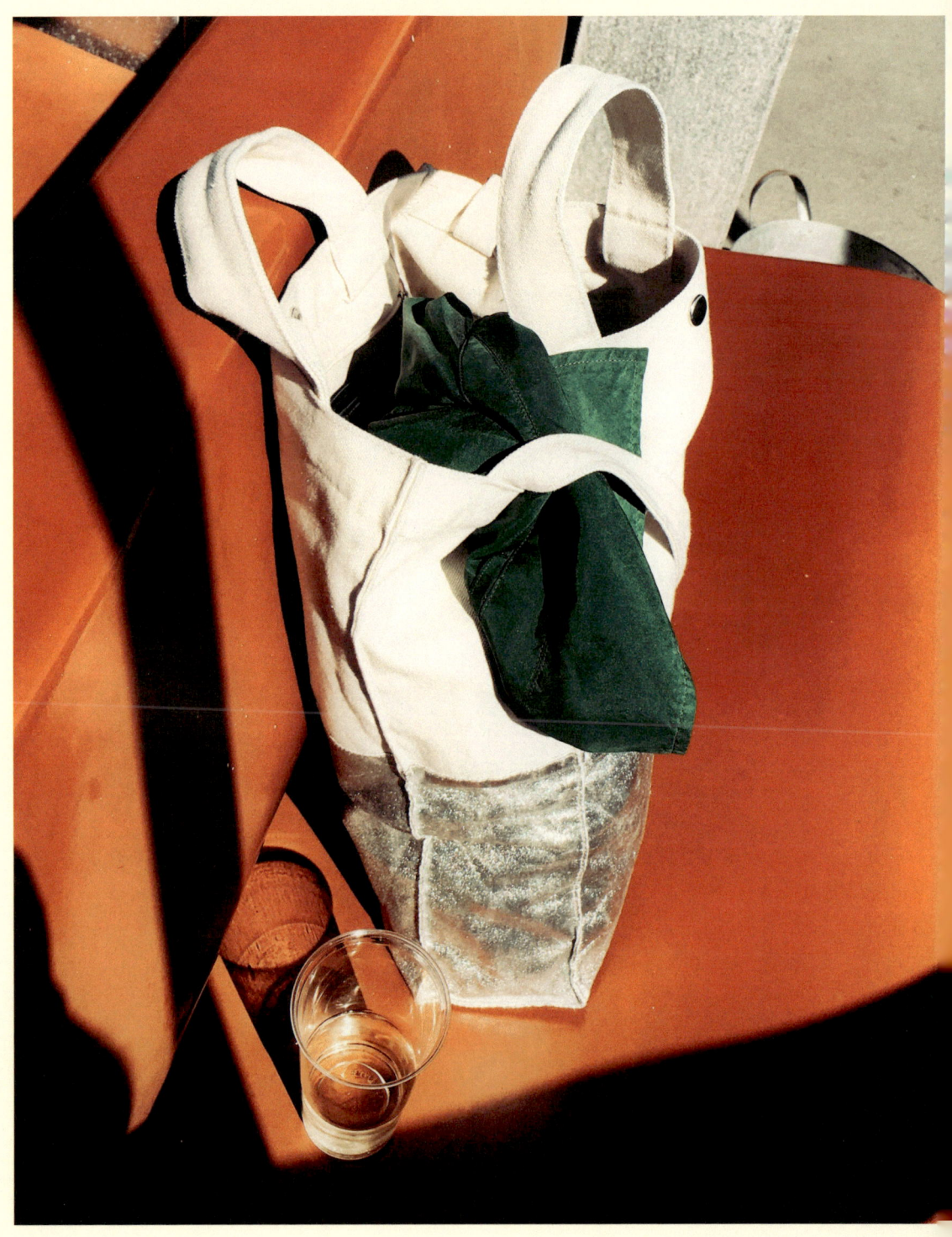

BEEN THERE, MYTHBUSTED THAT

Myth

DO YOU STILL HAVE A HUMAN RESOURCES DEPARTMENT?

Myth

DO YOU STILL HAVE A HUMAN RESOURCES DEPARTMENT?

Truth

TALENT MANAGEMENT AND ADOPT A NO LAYOFF POLICY

Historically, corporations were expected to serve some public purpose, justifying the benefits and privileges granted by the state. Many of these corporations offered lifelong employment and a pension for retirement. This paradigm shifted in the 1970s. Economist Milton Friedman contended that corporations have a sole responsibility to the shareholder. According to him, shareholders deserve 100% of profits minus taxes. Anything benefiting non-shareholders, or not aimed at ultimate profitability, amounts to misappropriation of shareholder funds. Friedman believed narrowing corporate focus to maximum profitability would enhance productivity and efficiency, thereby boosting economic growth and well-being.

At Million Dollar Baby, our objective is not to become a colossal enterprise or maximize profits. This can be a shocking answer when I ask groups of Christian business owners the question, "What is the purpose of a business?" Business, for me, is about serving all of our stakeholders lovingly through excellent products and services. That is the goal of our business, and profits are simply a validation of this goal being achieved.

According to our employees, we are one of the best workplaces in America with a Glassdoor score of 4.7. We love our employees and do our utmost to earn their love.

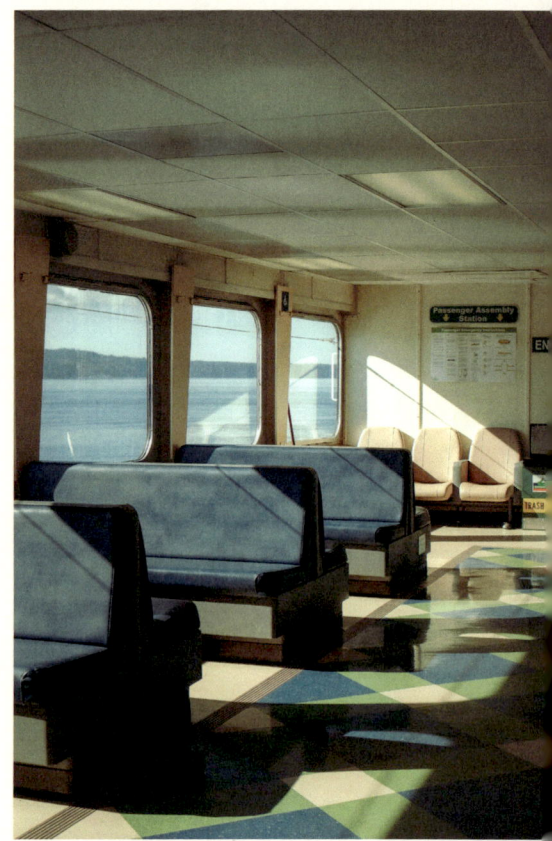

The largest single baby furniture factory in the world has only one customer: Million Dollar Baby. There is no contract for exclusivity; it is by choice that this factory has only selected us as a customer. We have been doing business with them for over thirty years. Million Dollar Baby once started as their smallest customer, and now we have numerous exclusive supplier relationships based on trust and a history of proven mutual profitability.

Our sales team's goal is to be the "first call" of our retailers. And we are. Instead of focusing on numeric goals, we strive to be the best problem solver in the market.

Finally, we strive for an average of 4.8 on all product ratings. Our goal is not to sell the most product in quantity but the best products in quality.

Even many Christian business owners cannot believe that making a profit is not our goal. They are businesses no different from secular ones except that they have incorporated Christian elements or sugar-coated their businesses with Christianity.

It can be even more shocking when I declare we have a no-layoff policy; we do not treat our employees as things that we can buy and discard at will. That is why, when I started the company in 1990, I coined the name Talent Management for our HR Department. Our company does not employ human resources; instead, it manages talented artists who will continuously create a new kind of business.

Of course, no company can simply declare a no-layoff policy without thinking this through deeply, thoroughly, and carefully. At my company, I have created a no-layoff fund that will pay all of our employees one year of salary, even if we have zero revenue. I believe it is unlikely we will ever reach a zero revenue scenario, but, if we do, we are prepared. I am confident one year would be enough time for us to turn things around and return to a healthy sales volume.

I have an example of putting this policy into practice. Once, in 2001, I had to shut down an entire business division in Hong Kong that handled denim fabric; it was no longer producing revenue, and I needed to shift focus to Million Dollar Baby. Yet I decided right then and there I was not going to lay off a single person. Instead, I utilized that team's talent to pivot and develop a new business. Today, that new division handles three key functions that are a vital part of our global operations.

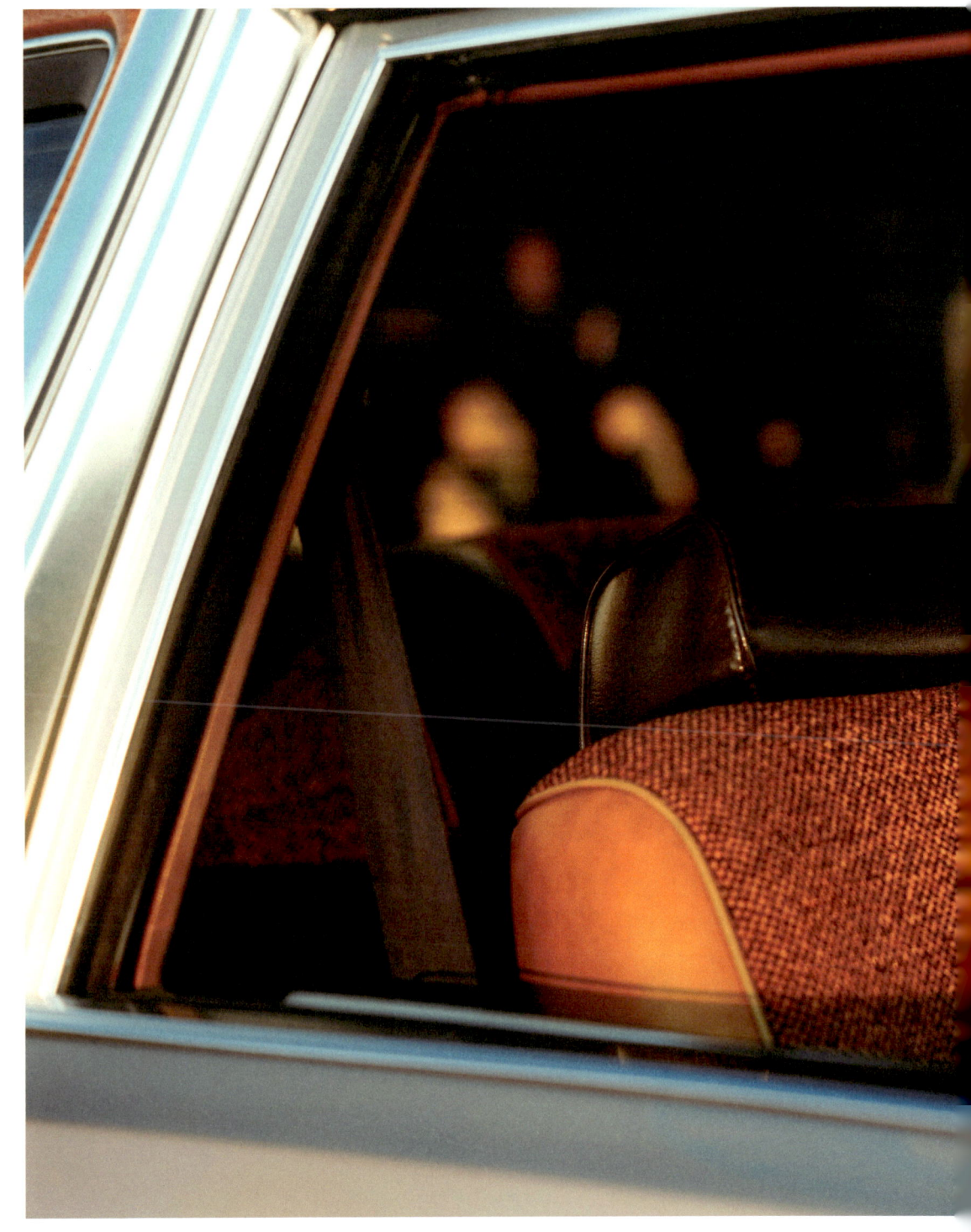

BEEN THERE, MYTHBUSTED THAT

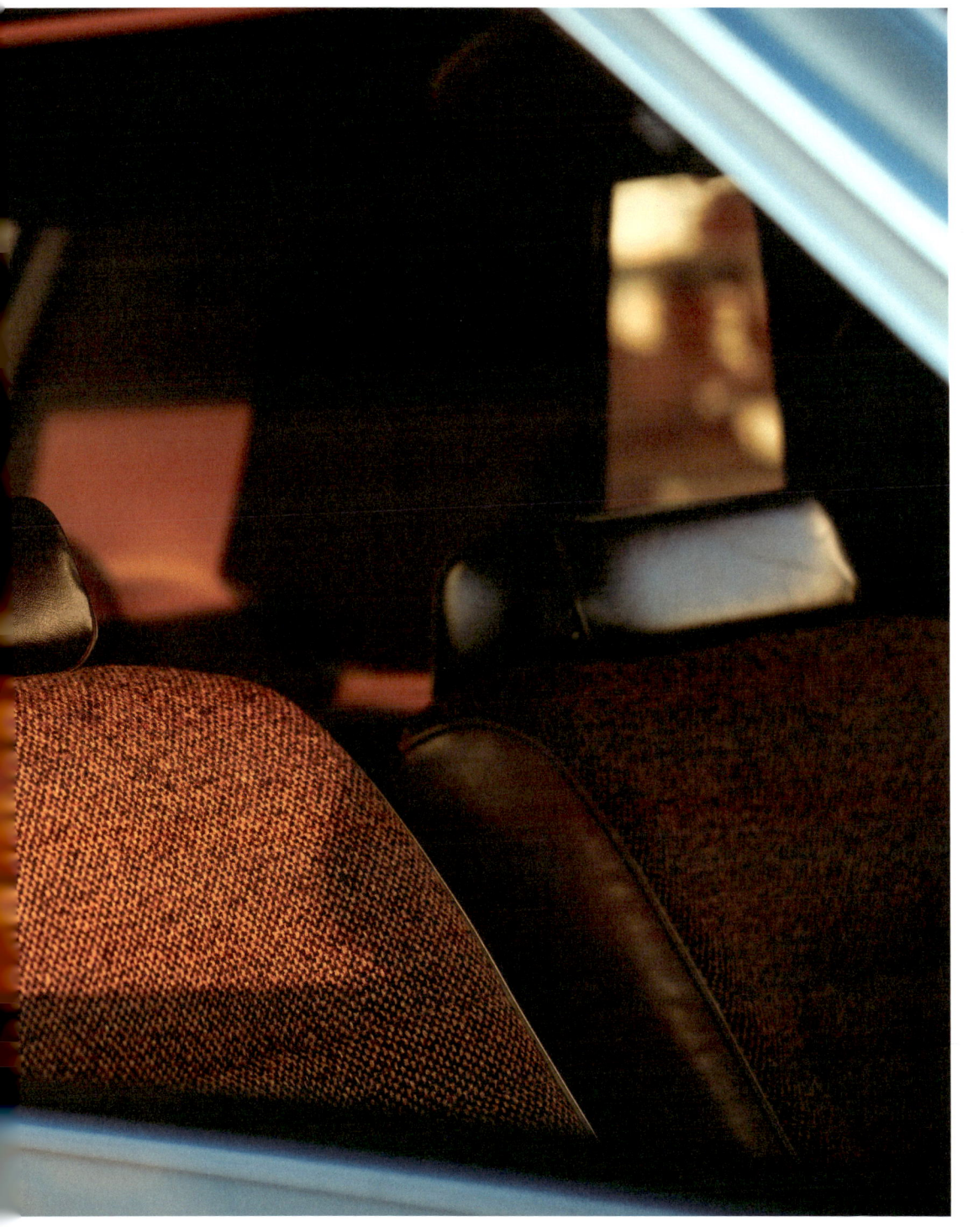

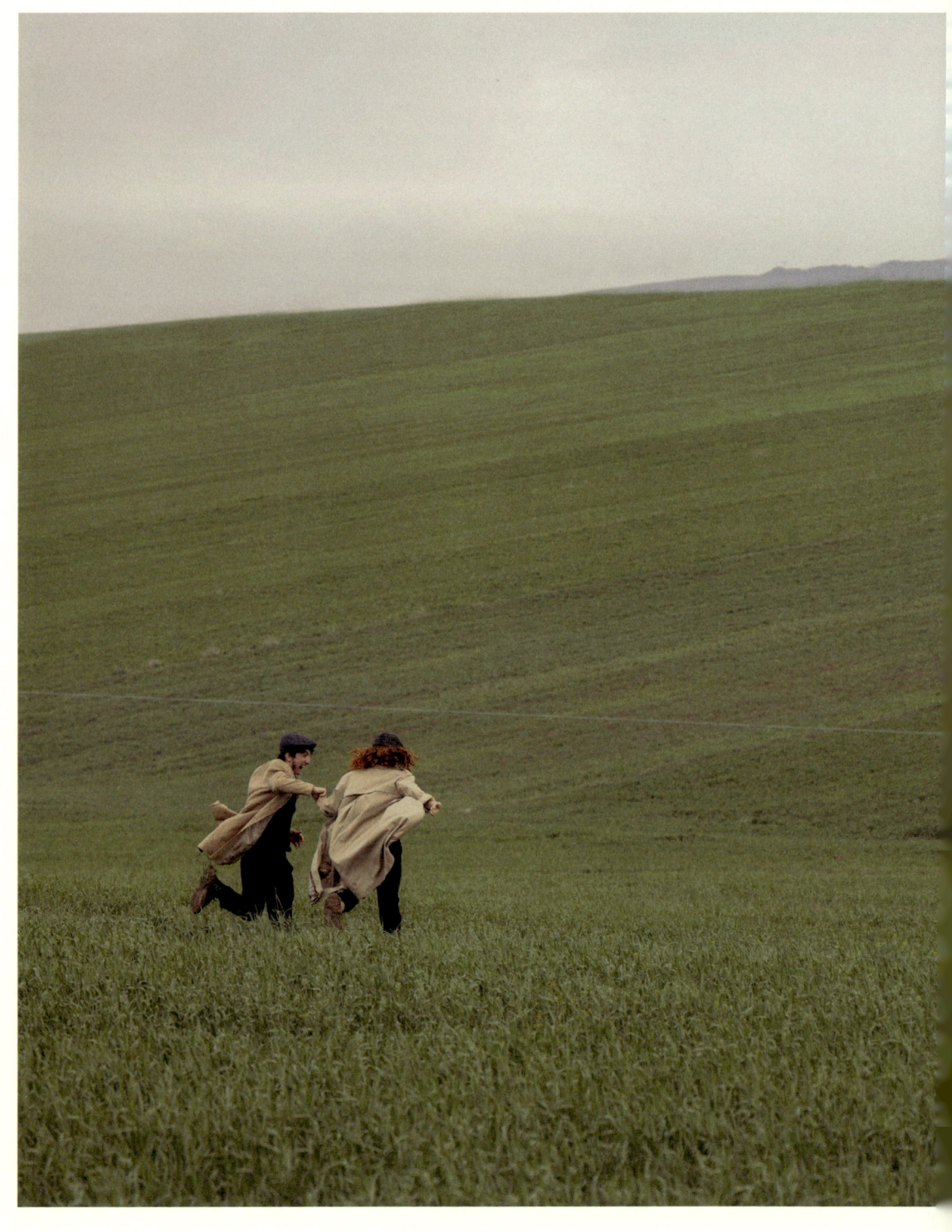

BEEN THERE, MYTHBUSTED THAT

Myth

COMPROMISE AND SACRIFICE ARE THE KEY TO A SUCCESSFUL MARRIAGE

Myth

Truth

ADOPT THE BIBLICAL PRACTICE OF TWO BECOME ONE

Genesis 2:24 eloquently states, "Therefore, a man shall leave his father and his mother and hold fast to his wife, and they shall become one flesh." This divine blueprint illustrates that marriage is a journey towards unity, where two distinct individuals are woven into a singular entity.

The path towards becoming one is no easy feat. Diverse personalities, life experiences, and cultural influences ensure that this journey is fraught with challenges. The individualistic nature of modern society complicates matters further, often placing personal desires above collective harmony. In this labyrinth, disagreements can serve as pivotal learning moments, offering insights into our partner's values and perspectives. These disagreements aren't about compromising or sacrificing; they are stepping stones to recalibrate and realign our shared values.

Conceiving a unified set of values and priorities necessitates collaborative effort fueled by love and mutual understanding. Instead of compromising or sacrificing, it is about molding and refining our individual biases into harmony. With this perspective, the journey is not a series of concessions; it is a transformative process wherein the old self gives way to the new.

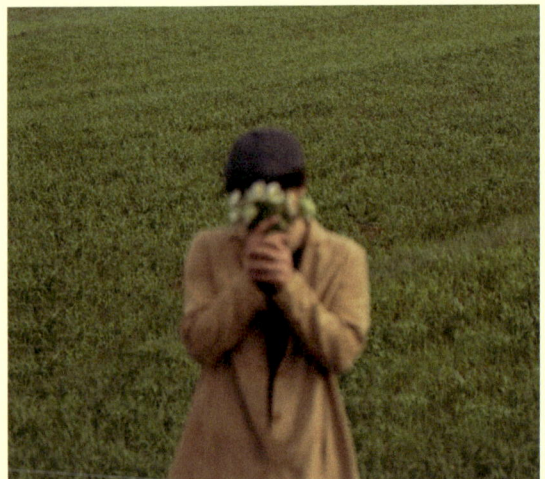

The prevailing notion in relationship advice is to compromise and sacrifice for a flourishing marriage. Yet, on closer examination, these strategies can lead to unintended consequences:

1. Compromises and sacrifices, while appearing as fair solutions, can create imbalances if not reciprocated. Resentment may brew, and buried needs can explode during heated arguments. There is an invisible balance sheet that receives entry every time one sacrifices. The list is always lopsided, and a detailed accounting will emerge during a heated argument, sounding something like: "Do you know how much and how many times I have sacrificed for you?"
2. These tactics provide temporary relief without addressing underlying issues. Silent agreements may avoid present conflicts but sow the seeds of future misunderstandings.
3. Persistent imbalances in sacrifices erode a relationship's equilibrium, fostering feelings of inequality and emotional distress.
4. Over time, depending solely on these strategies can drain joy and fulfillment, leaving partners feeling unfulfilled.

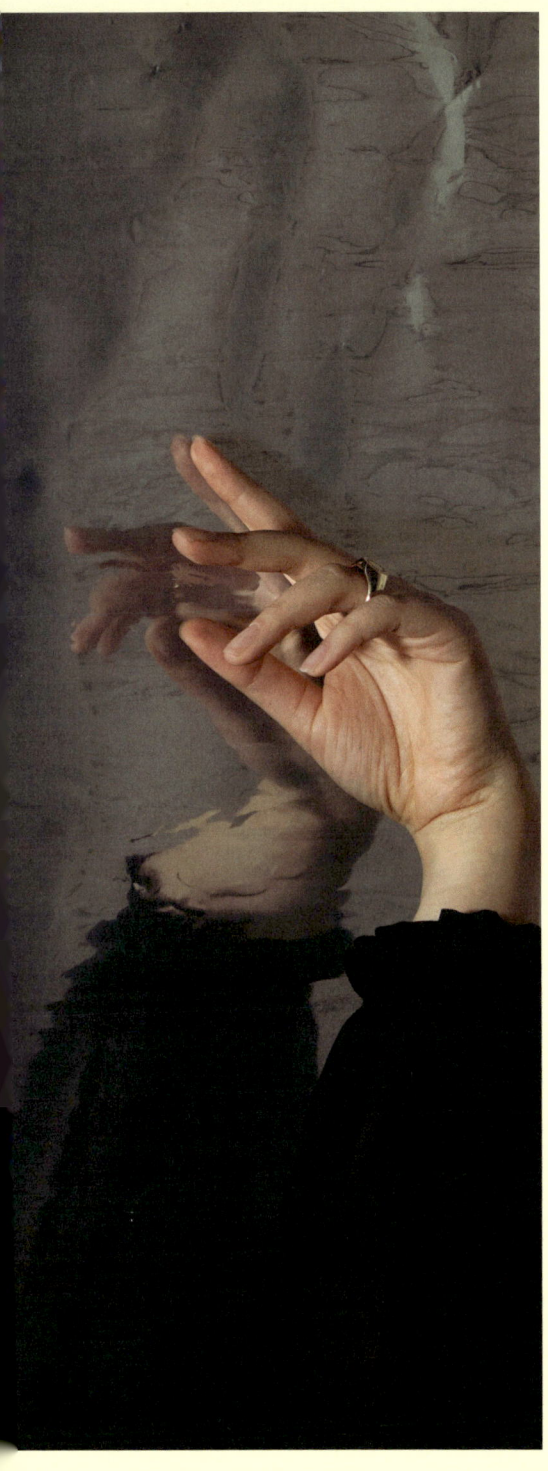

Drawing upon forty-three years of marriage, I propose a different approach:

1. Model marriage after the "two become one" paradigm, focusing on transparent communication and collaboration. Expressing needs, desires, and boundaries opens the door to new, mutually beneficial solutions.
2. Cherish individual contributions, harnessing them to support shared goals. Passion and pursuits align to create a formidable partnership.
3. The "two become one" process demands recalibration of individual biases into a unified perspective. This paradigm shift embodies the transformative journey advocated in the Bible.
4. Marriage transcends mere partnership; it is a union where two individuals blend into one cohesive entity. Embrace this union, or opt for individuality in singlehood.

It's important to emphasize that my perspective is rooted in faith and personal experiences. This passionate stance aims to stimulate reflection and provoke different perspectives compared to conventional views of marriage in society today.

Finally, marriage is not about discovering a perfect partner. The fallacy of perfection undermines true union. Instead, marriage is a journey of transformation and a testament to the miraculous design of the Divine. It isn't about finding perfection but evolving towards unity, creating a tapestry woven from the threads of shared growth and love.

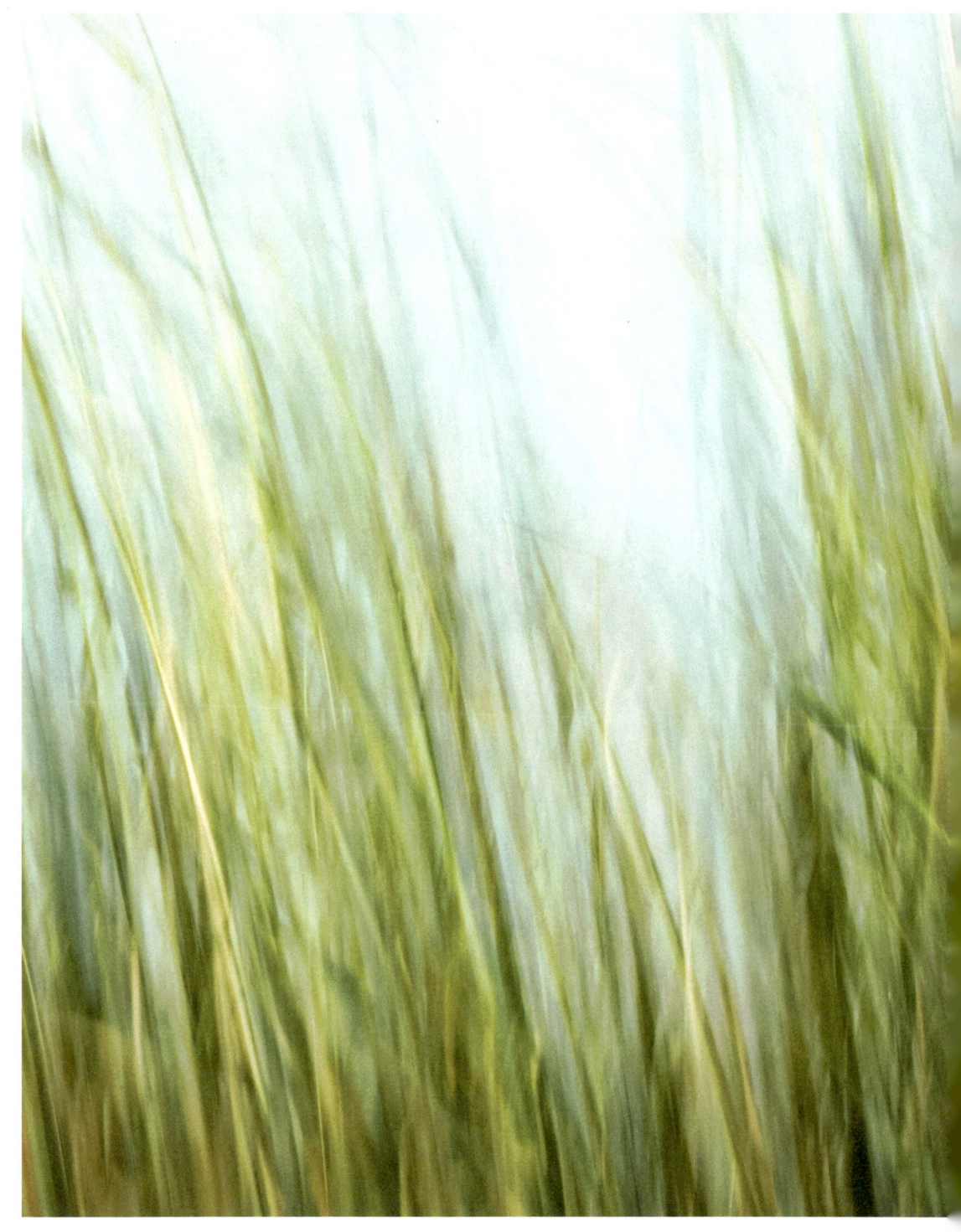

BEEN THERE, MYTHBUSTED THAT

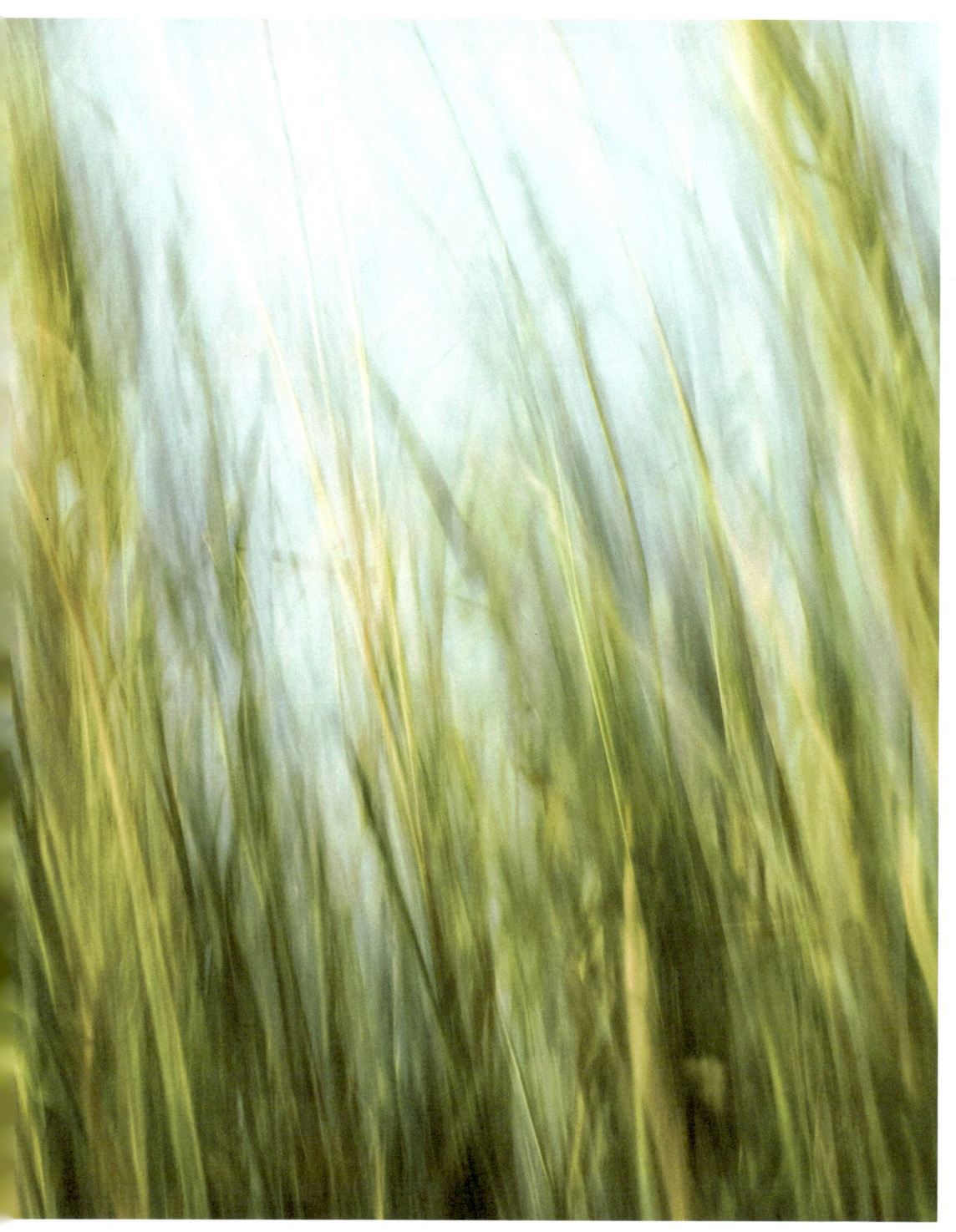

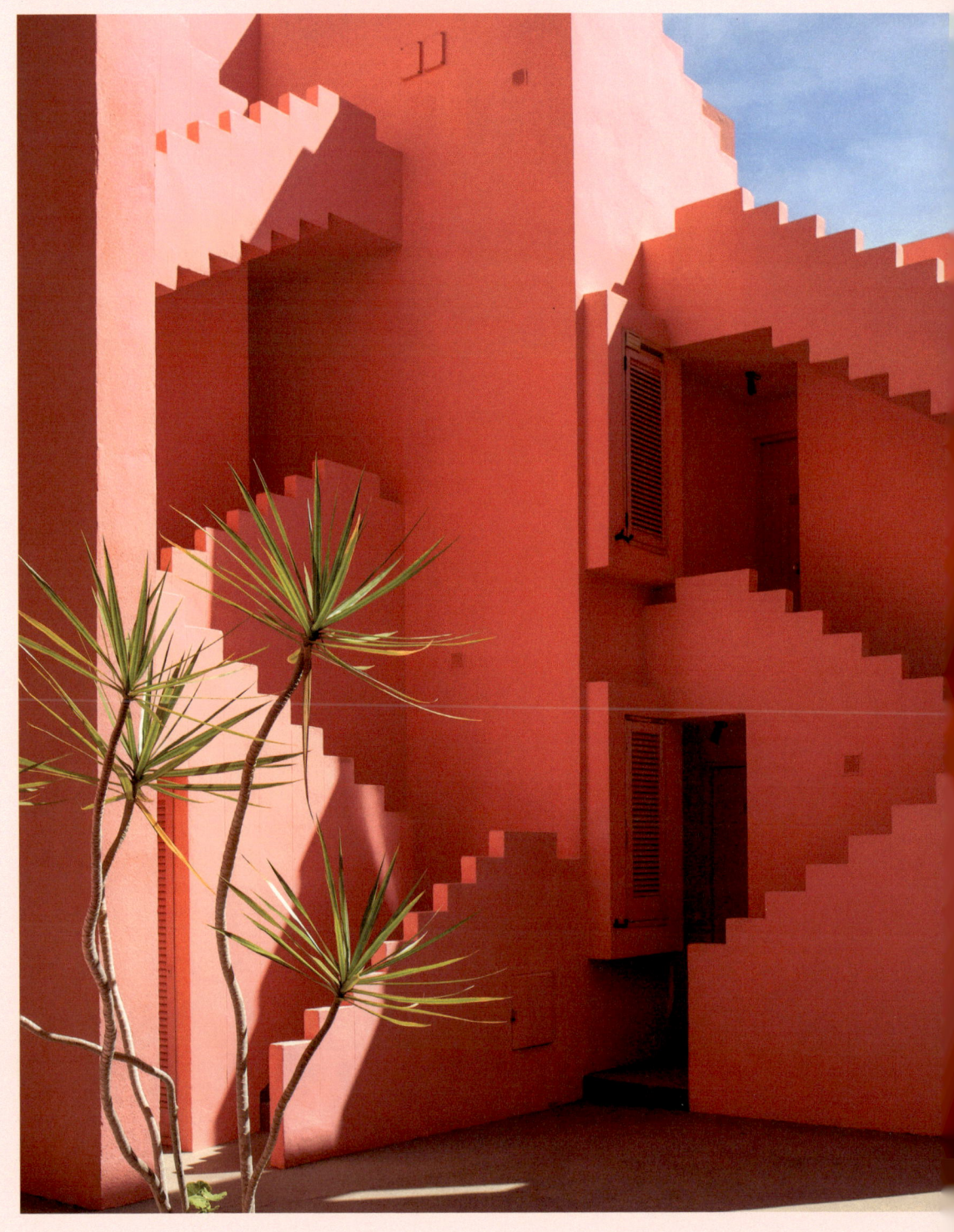

BEEN THERE, MYTHBUSTED THAT

Myth

FRUGALITY IS A VIRTUE

Truth

BE GENEROUS, ALWAYS

What is the difference between being generous and being frugal? They are two distinct approaches for handling resources, particularly finances.

Generosity vs Frugality

Definition

Generosity: the willingness to give, share, or provide resources, such as money, time, or possessions, to others without expecting something in return.

Frugality: the practice of being economical, thrifty, or careful in managing resources, particularly money, to avoid unnecessary spending.

Attitude

Generosity: often associated with an open-hearted and compassionate attitude, where individuals are willing to give sacrificially for the benefit of others.

Frugality: often associated with a mindset of prudence and self-discipline, where individuals carefully consider their spending choices to avoid wastefulness.

Focus

Generosity: centers on the desire to help others and make a positive impact on their lives or contribute to the well-being of a community or cause.

Frugality: centers on optimizing resource usage and minimizing expenses to save money and build financial security or achieve long-term financial goals.

Motivation

Generosity: the primary motivation for generosity is to make a difference in the lives of others, spread kindness, and express care and empathy.

Frugality: the primary motivation for frugality is to manage finances wisely, achieve financial independence, or accumulate savings for future needs or investments.

In essence, being generous involves a willingness to share resources for the benefit of others, driven by a compassionate and altruistic mindset. That is the biblical teaching to love thy neighbor as thyself. On the other hand, being frugal entails being mindful of resource usage, especially money, and making intentional choices to economize and avoid unnecessary expenses for personal financial stability and long-term goals. Therefore, frugality is more internally-focused.

But then, what is the difference between being frugal and being cheap? Based on my research, being frugal and being cheap are two distinct approaches to managing finances and spending money. While both involve being mindful of expenses, they differ significantly in their underlying motivations and the way they impact one's life and others around them.

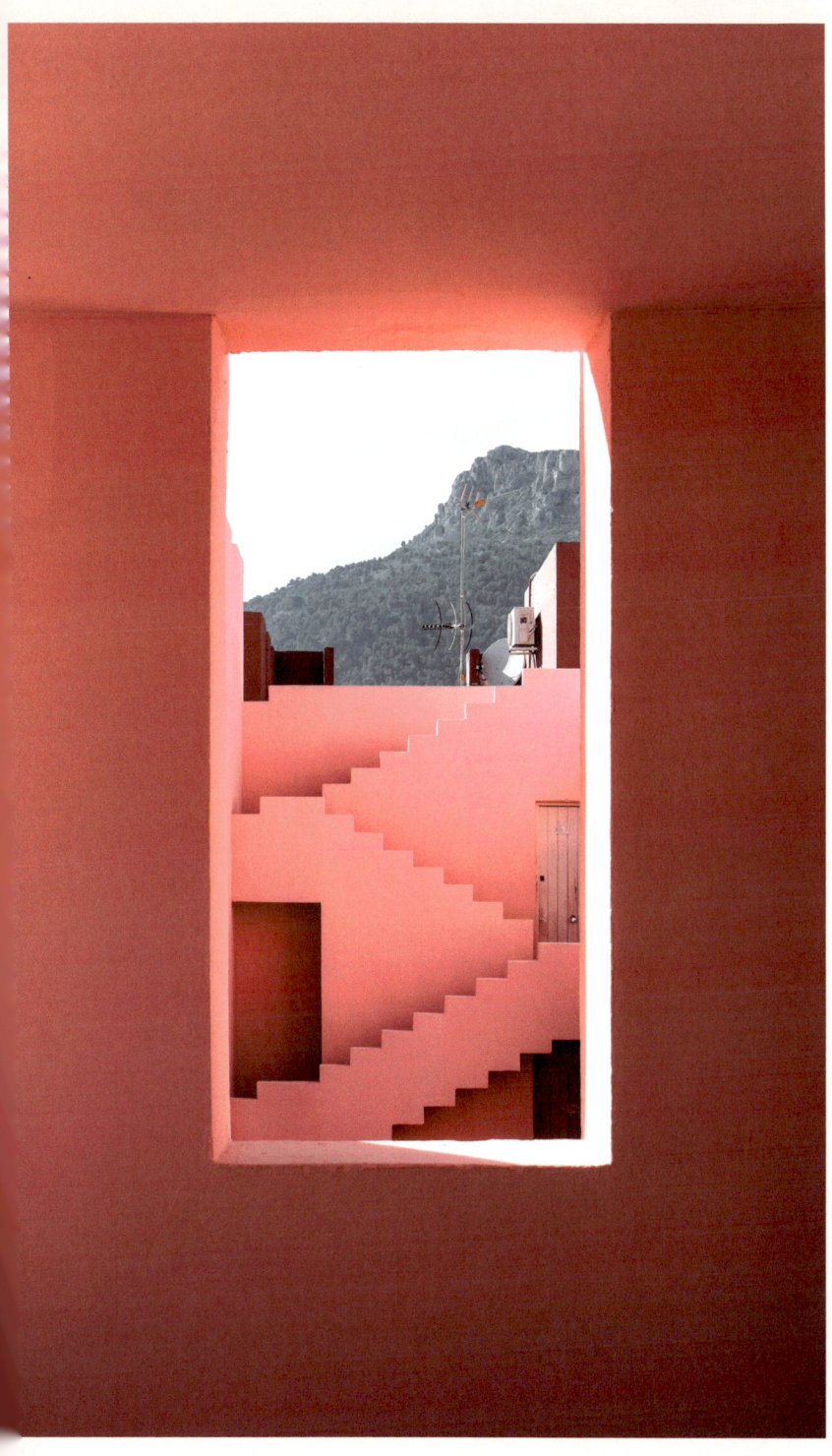

Frugality vs Cheapness

Motivation

Frugality: the primary motivation behind frugality is to make wise financial decisions and optimize resource usage. Frugal individuals aim to be prudent and economical without sacrificing quality or value. They focus on saving money for future needs and financial goals. This is considered a virtue in many cultures.

Cheapness: the primary motivation behind being cheap is to avoid spending money at all costs, often regardless of the impact on quality or value. Cheap individuals prioritize saving money over other considerations, even if it means compromising on essential needs or the well-being of others.

Approach to Spending

Frugality: frugal individuals carefully consider their purchases and seek value for their money. They may look for discounts, use coupons, or wait for sales to get the best deals on quality products or services.

Cheapness: cheap individuals are more likely to cut corners, seek the absolute lowest prices, and prioritize the cheapest option, even if it means sacrificing quality or convenience.

Impact on Quality of Life

Frugality: aims to strike a balance between saving money and maintaining a reasonable quality of life. Frugal individuals are willing to spend on items or experiences that align with their values and contribute to their overall well-being.

Cheapness: being cheap often leads to a lower quality of life. Cheap individuals may avoid necessary expenses, opt for inferior products or services, or miss out on opportunities to improve their overall happiness and satisfaction.

Impact on Others

Frugality: frugal individuals are mindful of their financial responsibilities but are also willing to be generous when appropriate. They can consider the needs and feelings of others and may be willing to spend funds on shared experiences or give thoughtful gifts.

Cheapness: being cheap can have a negative impact on others as it may result in unwillingness to contribute to group expenses or share the burden of costs in social or family settings.

Long-Term Perspective

Frugality: often comes with a long-term perspective, focusing on saving and building financial security for the future.

Cheapness: tends to be short-sighted, prioritizing immediate savings over long-term financial well-being or the quality of life.

For me, the key difference between being frugal and being cheap lies in the underlying motivation. From my observation and coaching sessions with young people, very few people can manage the slippery slope between frugality and cheapness deliberately and in most cases, end up being cheap without being conscious of it. Instead of pointing the finger towards other people, let us all review our own examples of our own unconsciousness when navigating that slippery slope.

My advice to mentees is to forget about frugality and focus more on generosity. Err on the side of being more generous instead of being an expert in frugality. To me, being overly generous to the point of bankruptcy is not a slippery slope. I have not known any people like that, and I challenge you to name one. Being foolish in financial management is not being generous.

Of course, I am speaking from a position of privilege, blessings, and wealth, but I am giving advice also to people of privilege—including my own family and clan. It is difficult for me to see why wealthy people still strive to be frugal. While being generous is about more than just money, being frugal and cheap are mindsets all about money.

Following the same train of thought, to me, problems solvable by money are not problems if there is enough money to be deployed. Real problems are not solvable by money, and we can all name examples of problems that money cannot solve, no matter how wealthy one is. So, is being frugal a good practice? Are you aware of how many marriages have been ruined because of frugality?

Here is another idea: money not spent is not wealth. It is only a number in your bank account. Money is a tool. It is not an asset if we do not put it to good use. Likewise, our talents and gifts are only assets if we put them into good use. Theologically, we are stewards of God's blessings. A steward deploys assets for the benefits of the marginalized, which is God's will and command. It relaxes me when I no longer view money as my possession.

Another way to think about this subject is a mindset of abundance versus scarcity. Instead of focusing on saving by being frugal—a scarcity mindset—I want to be in a position of continuous production of assets, including money—an abundance mindset—and give generously for the benefit of the marginalized. The expression of the continuous production of assets is the practice of continuous learning and continuous improvement, rather than constantly trying to pursue a means to an end.

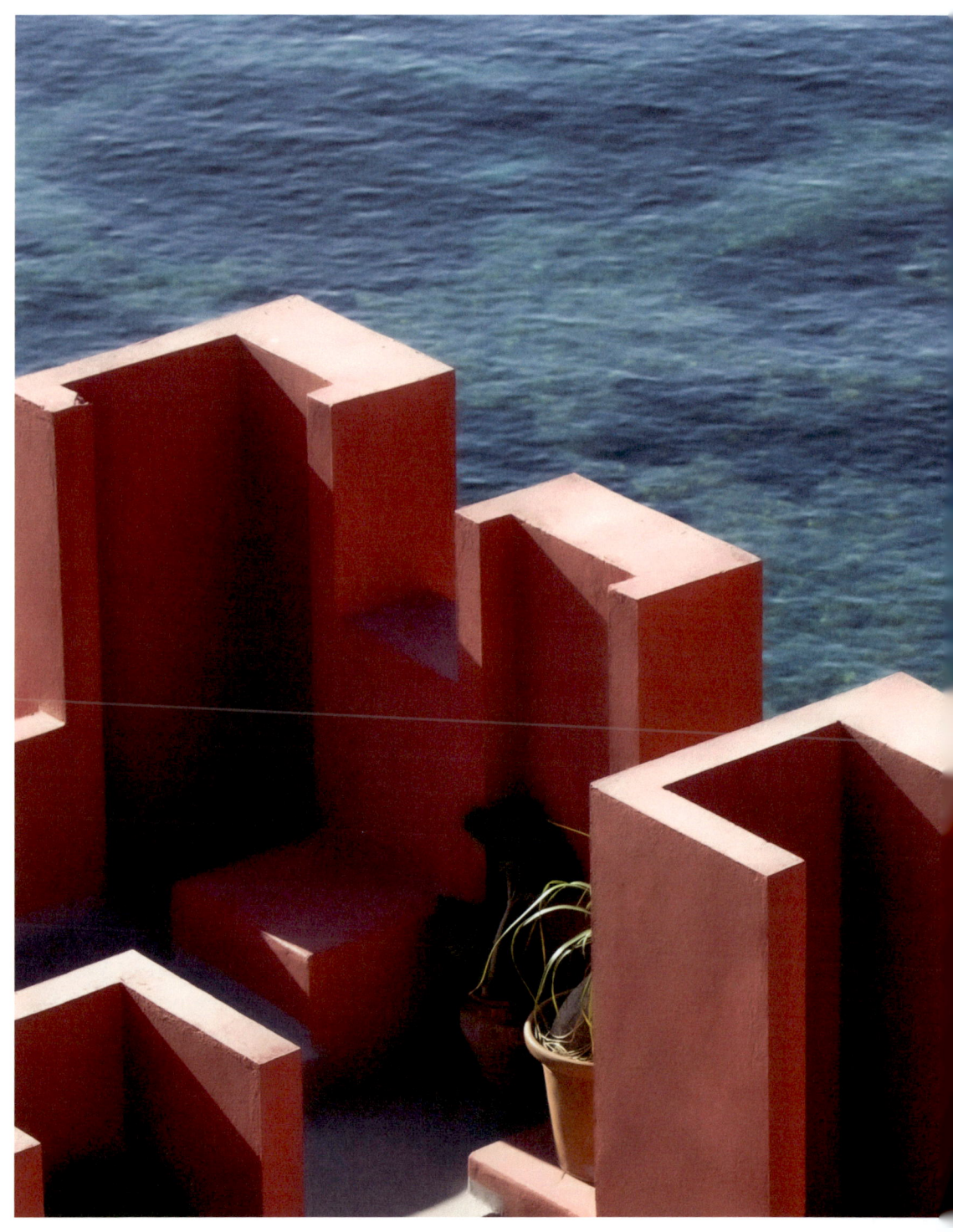

BEEN THERE, MYTHBUSTED THAT

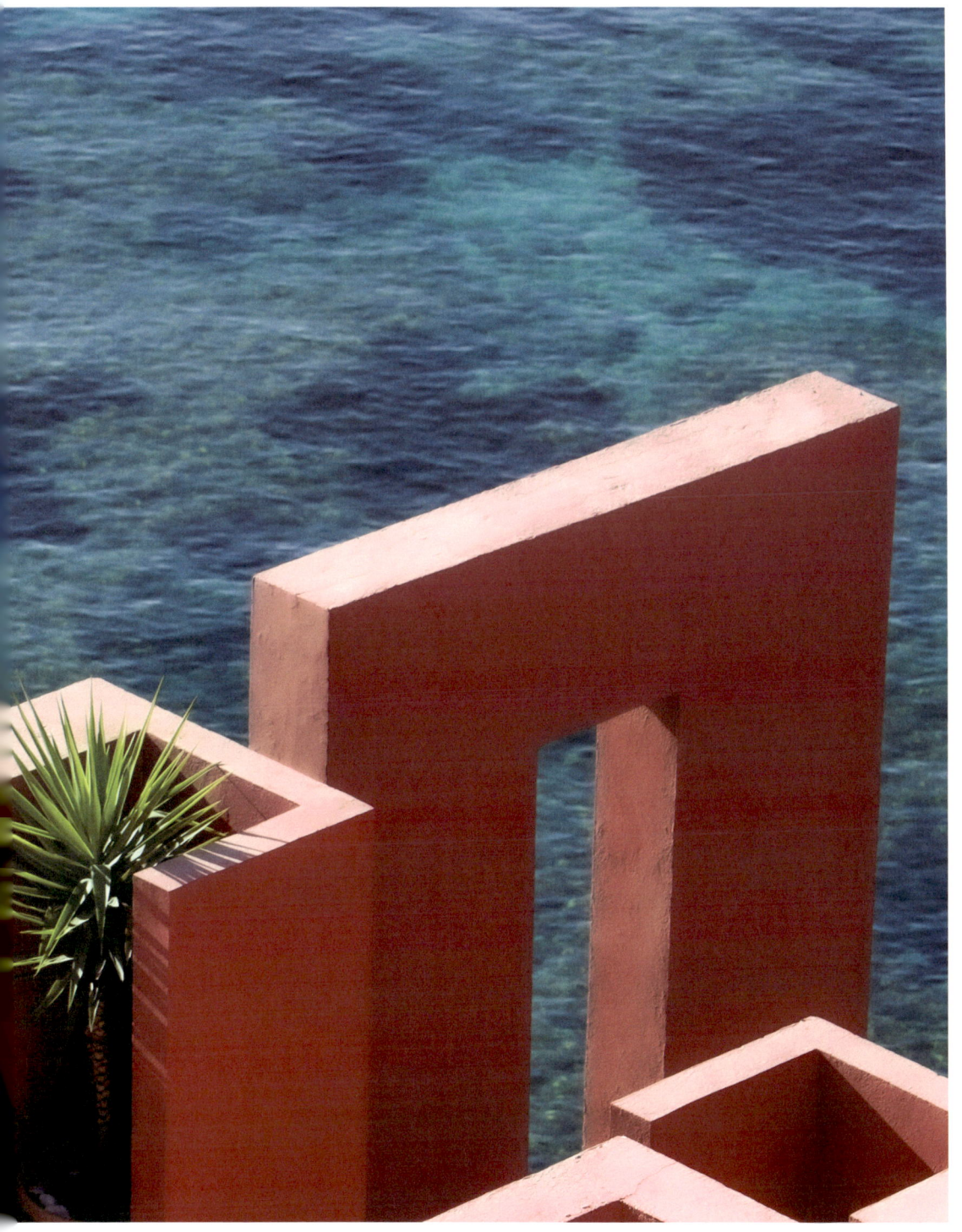

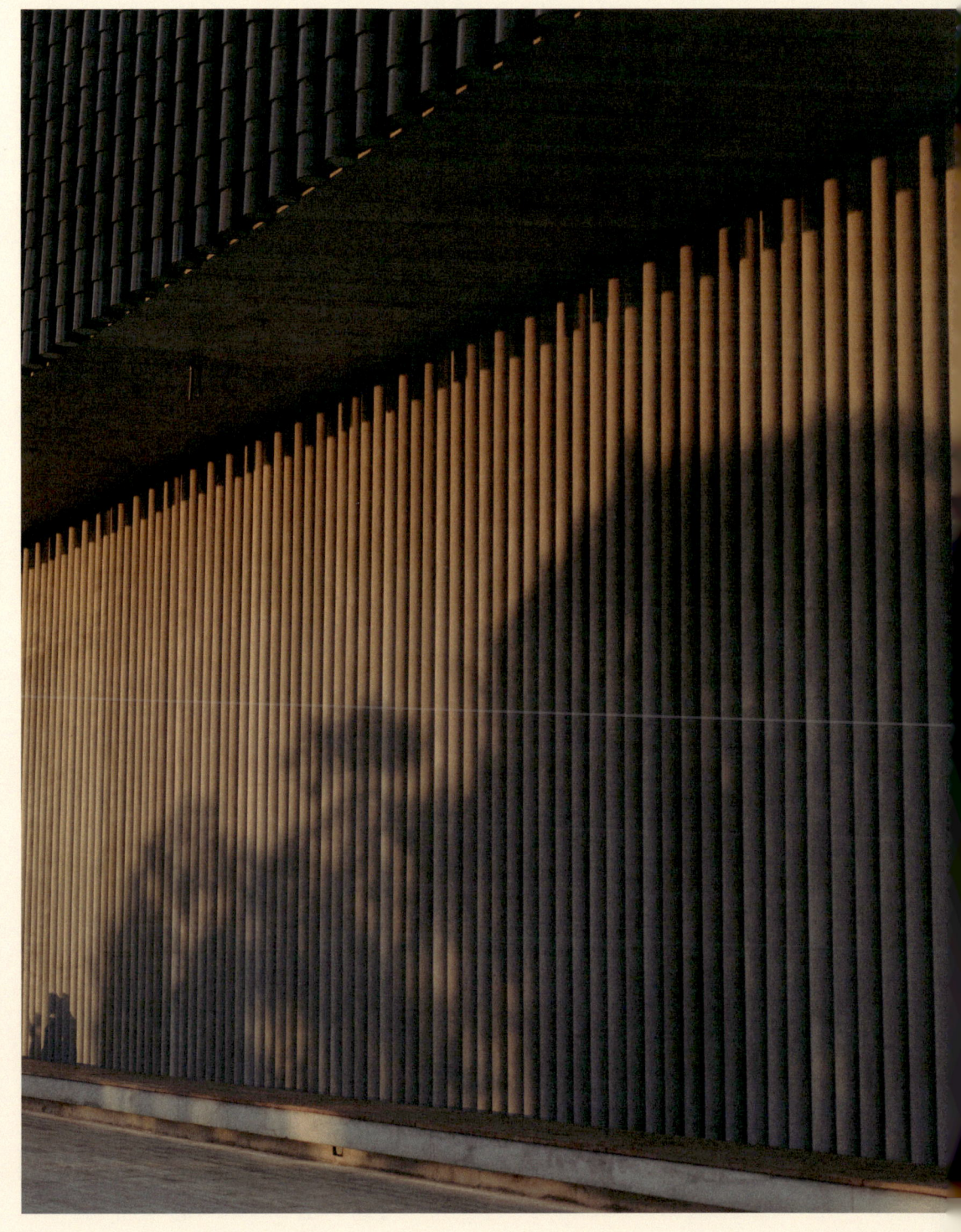

BEEN THERE, MYTHBUSTED THAT

Myth

FOCUS ON YOUR LEGACY IN ORDER TO FINISH WELL

Truth

FORGET ABOUT OUR LEGACY AND FOCUS ON GENERATIONAL TRANSITION

Legacy & Generational Transfer

Bearing the mantle of a resolute Chinese patriarch, it is a notable exception to have handed over my CEO position to my son since November 2015, three years before my sixtieth birthday. As in each choice I make, the decision was guided by my theology.

When Maryann was recovering from colon cancer surgery, my daughter, Tracy, chose to join Million Dollar Baby to fill her mother's role rather than pursuing a career in New York City after graduating from college. I remember that, on Tracy's first day in the office, many employees felt refreshed by her demeanor and conduct. It was a realization of how invigorating it is to collaborate with someone profoundly

intelligent and dedicated. Tracy's connection with the industry and company grew, and she transformed her temporary role into a long-term commitment.

As Tracy and her younger brother, Teddy, grew up, I repeatedly emphasized that there was no pressure for them to enter the family business. I encouraged them to carve out their own unique paths, just as I did. I made it clear that there was no pressure to join the family business and, also, that sharing the Fong surname did not automatically guarantee them a Vice President title if they decided to enter the company. They would be welcomed but would begin where every employee must start: at the bottom.

Given my exceptional experience working with Tracy and her positive influence on the company, I decided it was time to "recruit" my son into the business as well. I did not change my original philosophy; I did not mandate or demand that he enter the business. Instead, I followed a standard recruitment process like any other company. During spring break of Teddy's senior year at Harvard, I brought Teddy and two of his classmates from Boston to Los Angeles. We conducted a company tour, outlined the company's vision, and offered them all trainee positions. Our family was blessed yet again—this recruitment endeavor succeeded, and all three Harvard graduates joined Million Dollar Baby.

When Million Dollar Baby was founded thirty-three years ago in 1990, one of my brothers-in-law and one of my sisters were among the first seven employees. After Tracy and Teddy joined, our small company boasted a team of six family members. Despite our kinship, we faced challenges and did not always manage projects perfectly. Still, our primary goal, echoing our commitment to glorify God through daily excellence, included fostering harmonious collaboration within the family for the greater glory of God.

Guided by the Holy Spirit, I initiated quarterly meetings outside the workplace for family members in the business. These meetings commenced in December 2012, and I invited a long-time family friend and former mentor to guide these sessions. During our inaugural meeting, I estab-

lished that the ultimate objective of our business was to glorify God through our excellence. We would utilize these family meetings as a platform to address familial issues, sparing arguments in front of other employees during regular working hours. In the presence of fellow employees, our family should present a united front. What sets our family apart is our unique approach. Most other family businesses, regardless of their size, have extensive rules for family member interactions. These rules primarily aim to safeguard the business from disruption by unsuitable family members. Instead, during our initial meeting, after emphasizing the principle of glorifying God, Maryann chimed in, stating that after God, family comes first. She asserted that if our family couldn't cooperate, resolve disputes, and work harmoniously and excellently together, then we should be prepared to close the business. This encounter expresses the impor-

tance of family and the potential for healthy boundaries within a business.

During that initial meeting, it occurred to me to discuss the issue of legacy and transition, particularly for myself. Although I was only fifty-four years old at the time, I recognized the importance of foresight and direction. It was decided, with Tracy's blessing, that Teddy would become the next CEO. Because we all felt that he was not quite ready at that point, he would begin his training with me and we became co-CEOs.

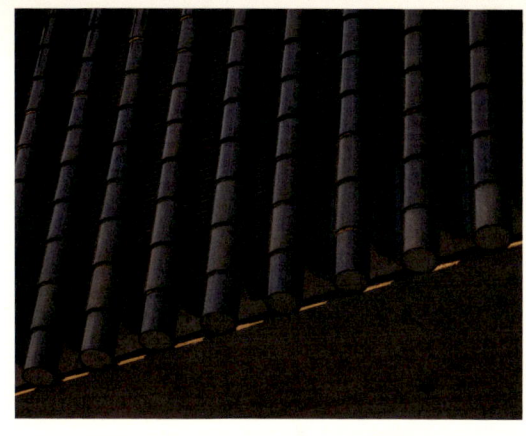

This transitional process sets us apart from what I have read or observed elsewhere. In Hong Kong, most prominent families are entangled in legal battles among their members. Many big companies face challenges when transitioning from one CEO to the next. My observation led me to the conclusion that the notion of "legacy"—the desire to pass on and preserve what one generation deems best—is the root cause of many problems. As a devout follower of Christ, I understand that I do not possess anything on this Earth. Jesus taught us not to accumulate treasures here but to focus on eternal treasures. We are merely stewards, managing the talents and assets God has entrusted to us. Our task is to glorify God through this responsible stewardship. Consequently, we shouldn't adopt an ownership mentality but, instead, embody a dedicated servant mindset, encouraging the next generation to pave their own path as we transition our assets (in all aspects) to them. How does this translate to the Fong family transition, from me to my son? When I declared Teddy as my co-CEO in Novem-

ber 2013, I conveyed the following at our quarterly company-wide meeting: I believe that an excellent CEO inherently imprints their own personality and beliefs onto a company's culture. Expecting a new CEO to maintain the same culture as the previous one can be a pitfall for esteemed companies. Think of the "IBM way" or the "HP Hewlett-Packard way." While they were effective for a specific era, these models had to evolve or be discarded to steer the companies toward survival. Therefore, I declared that under Teddy's stewardship the culture of Million Dollar Baby would change—and rightly so. Teddy should be empowered and encouraged to make the changes he deems necessary. I did not burden him with a list of immutable aspects or unchanging principles. I also supported him in assembling his own team. With the help of family members as a crucial part of that leadership team, Million Dollar Baby has tripled in size since Teddy became the new CEO.

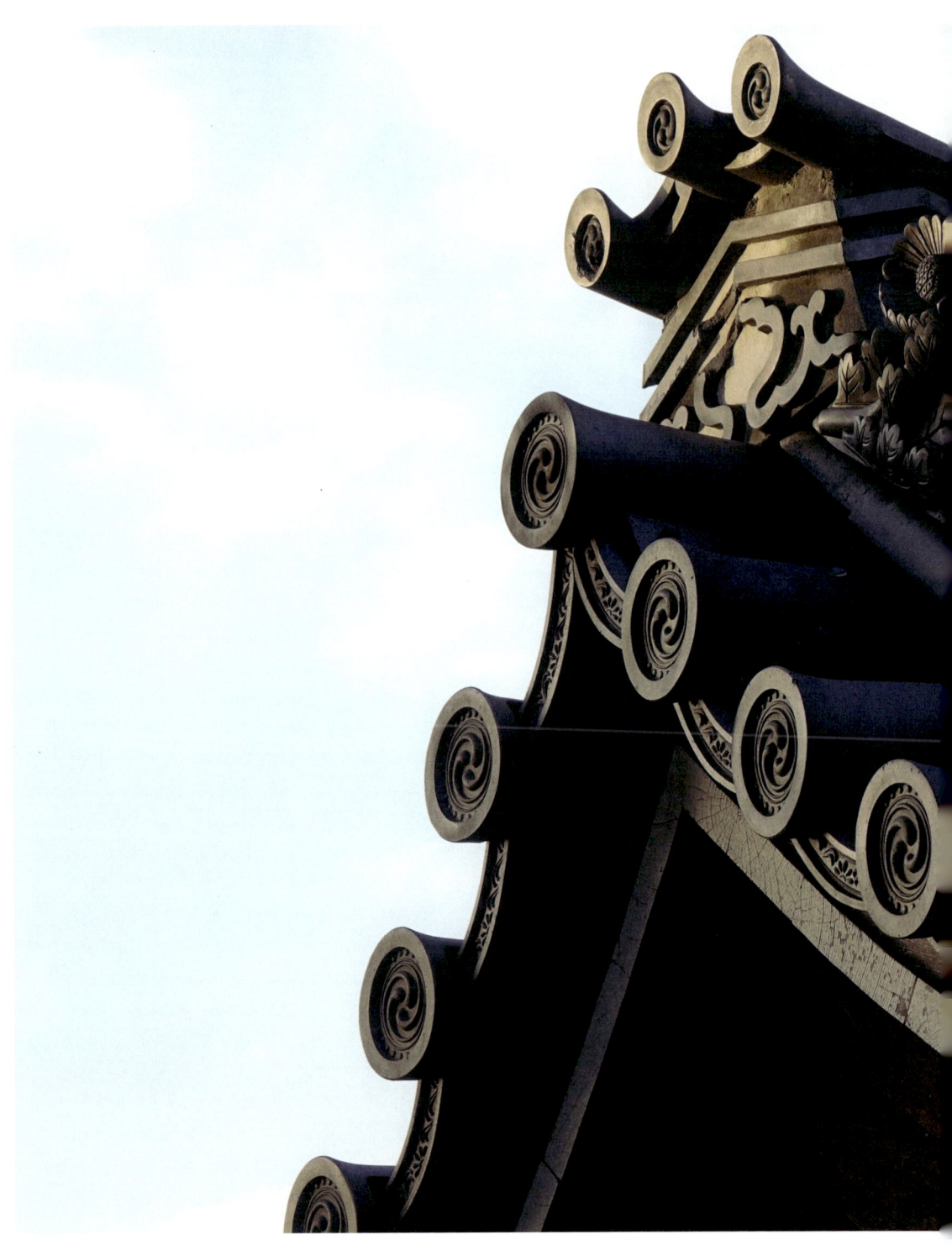

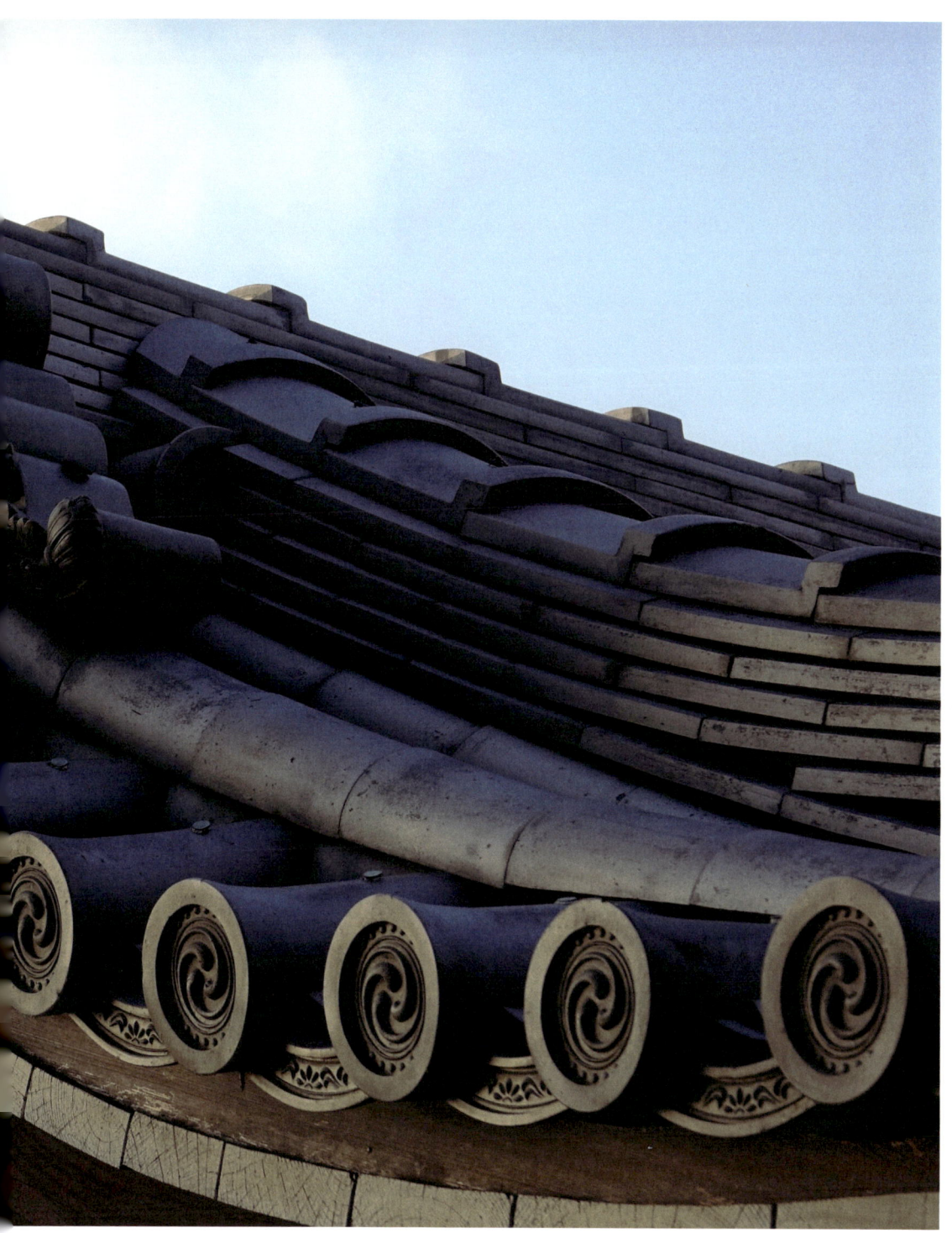

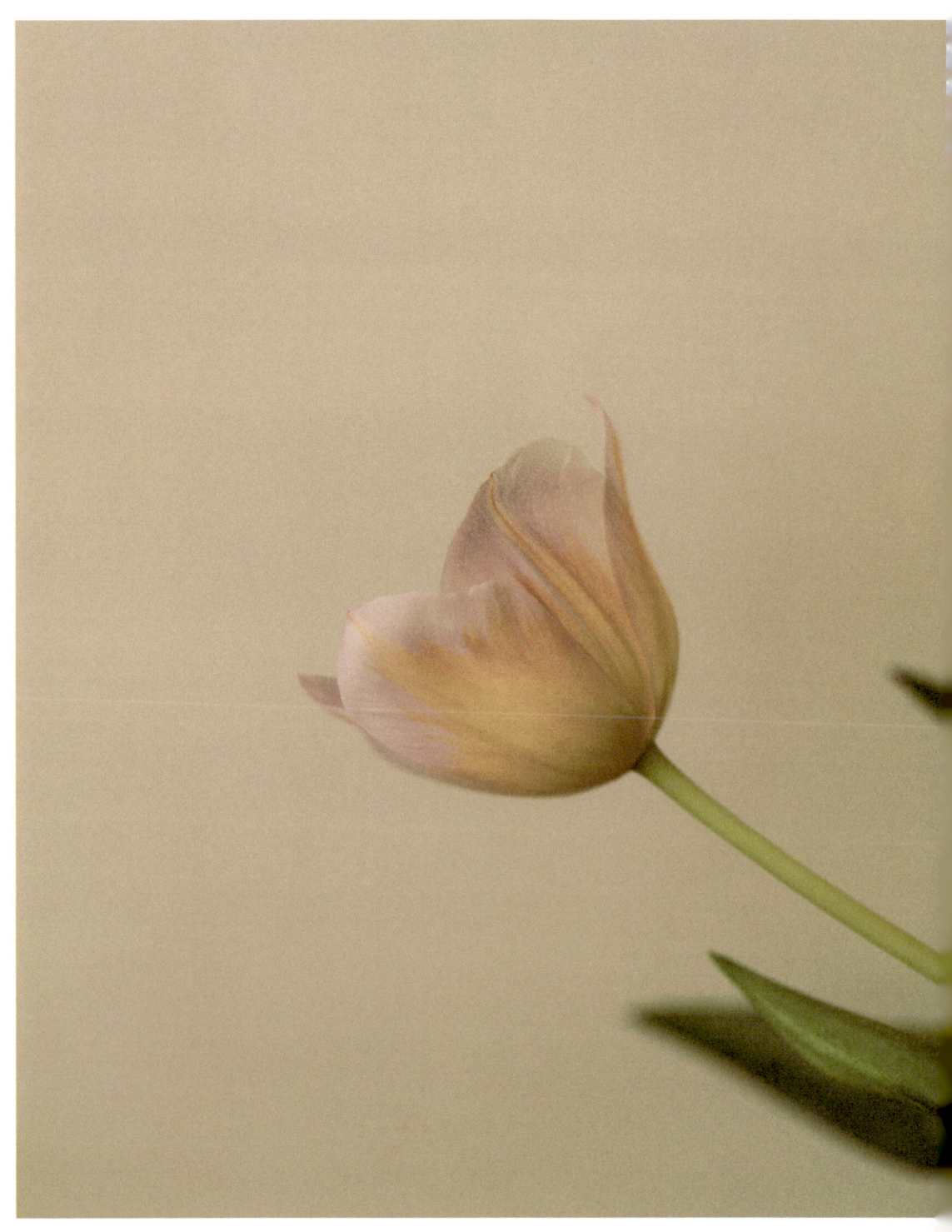

BEEN THERE, MYTHBUSTED THAT

Myth

EQUAL PERCENTAGES EXPRESS EQUAL LOVE

MAJORITY SHARE TO THE MOST COMPETENT AND RESPONSIBLE

I do not believe in 50/50 partnerships. It may work when the company or organization is small and close to bankruptcy; in these cases, there is simply no time for argument with a sole focus on survival. However, when abundant money and egos are involved, the assumption that two people can always come to an agreement is a myth.

In Asia, particularly in Hong Kong, it is common for members of wealthy families to sue each other. The problems of the younger generations arise from the results of poor planning by the older generation before passing away.

A famous Hong Kong roast goose restaurant closed because of these types of problems. The father, for the sake of being "fair," divided the shares of the restaurant equally amongst his three children. The two younger siblings, who never worked at the restaurant, were not interested in tying up all their assets in the business. They forced a liquidation from the older brother, who had always been a part of the business but only owned one third of the shares. It was sad to see, and this is not an isolated example.

Older generations blame younger generations for the eruption of family feuds and bemoan that family wealth never lasts three generations. The myth here is that younger generations cannot live up to the grit and perseverance of the previous generation and end up becoming spoiled. But who is responsible for spoiling them in the first place? The next generation is a direct reflection of the values, beliefs, and morals of the previous generation. If the next generation fails (by whatever definition you want to ascribe to that word), then the previous generation must bear that responsibility.

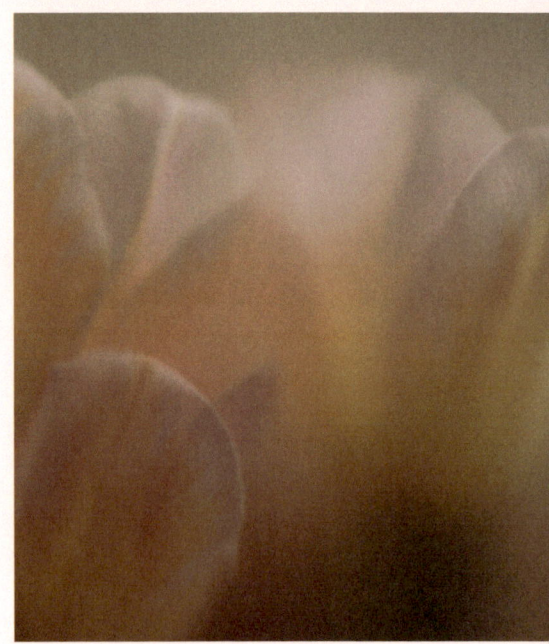

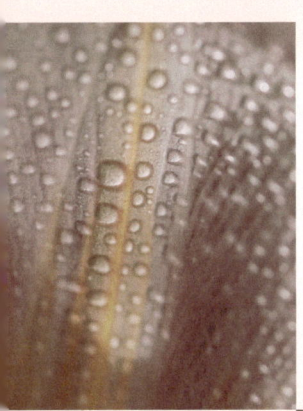

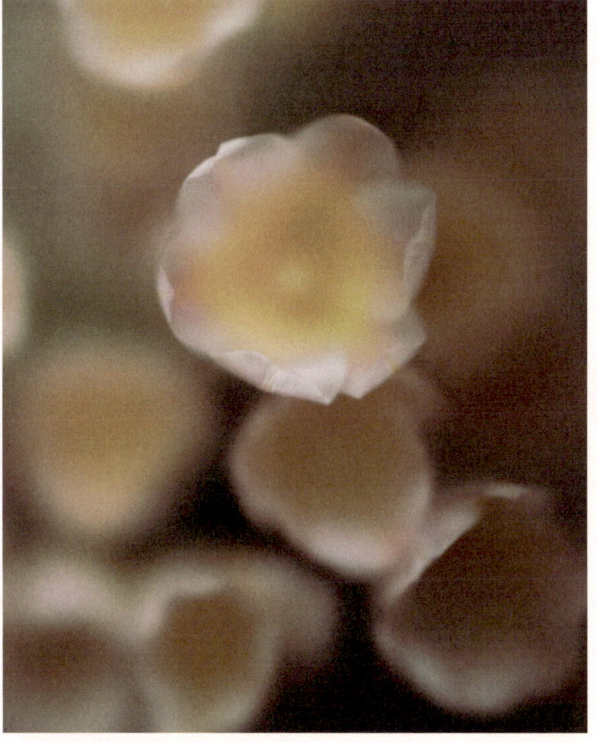

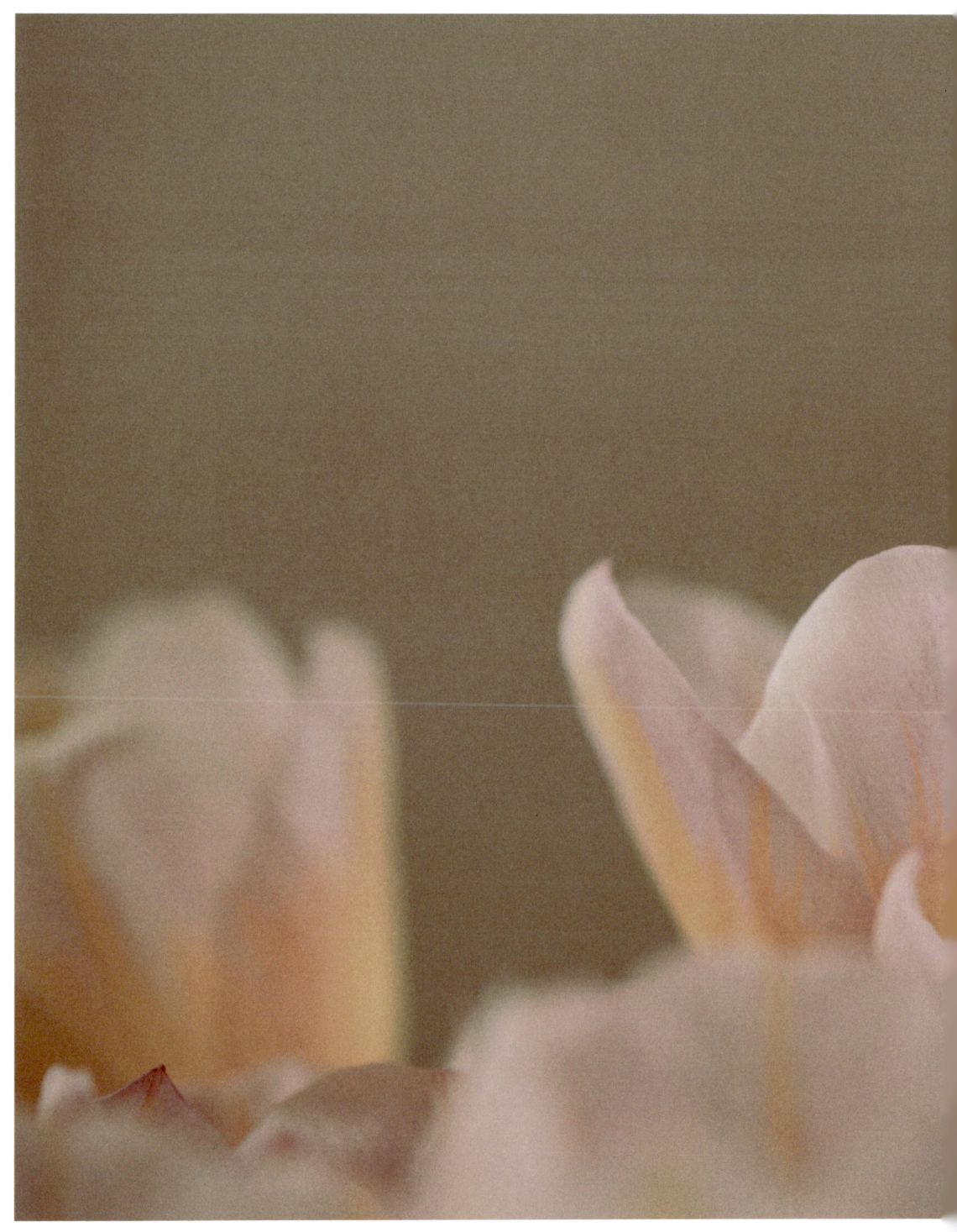

BEEN THERE, MYTHBUSTED THAT

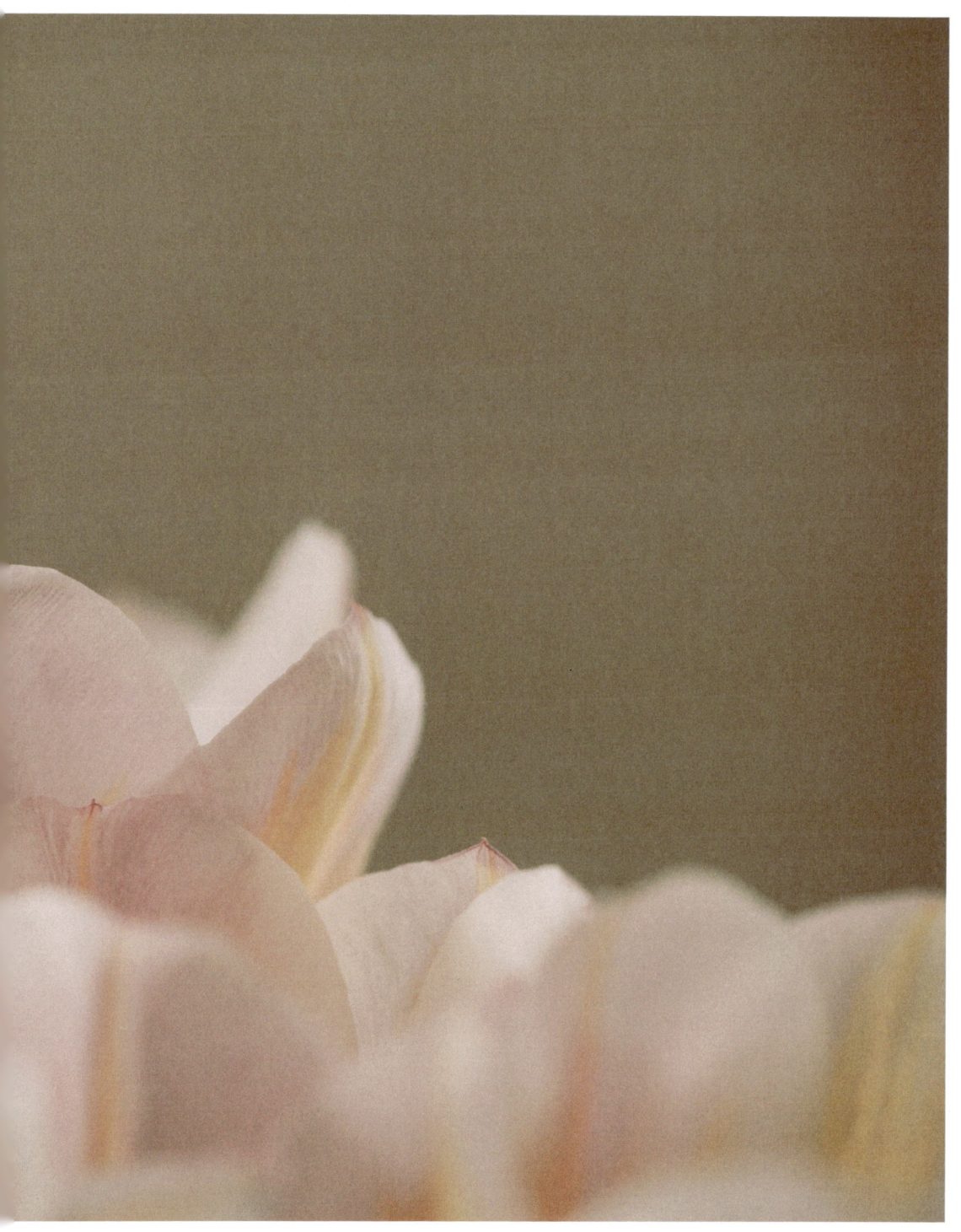

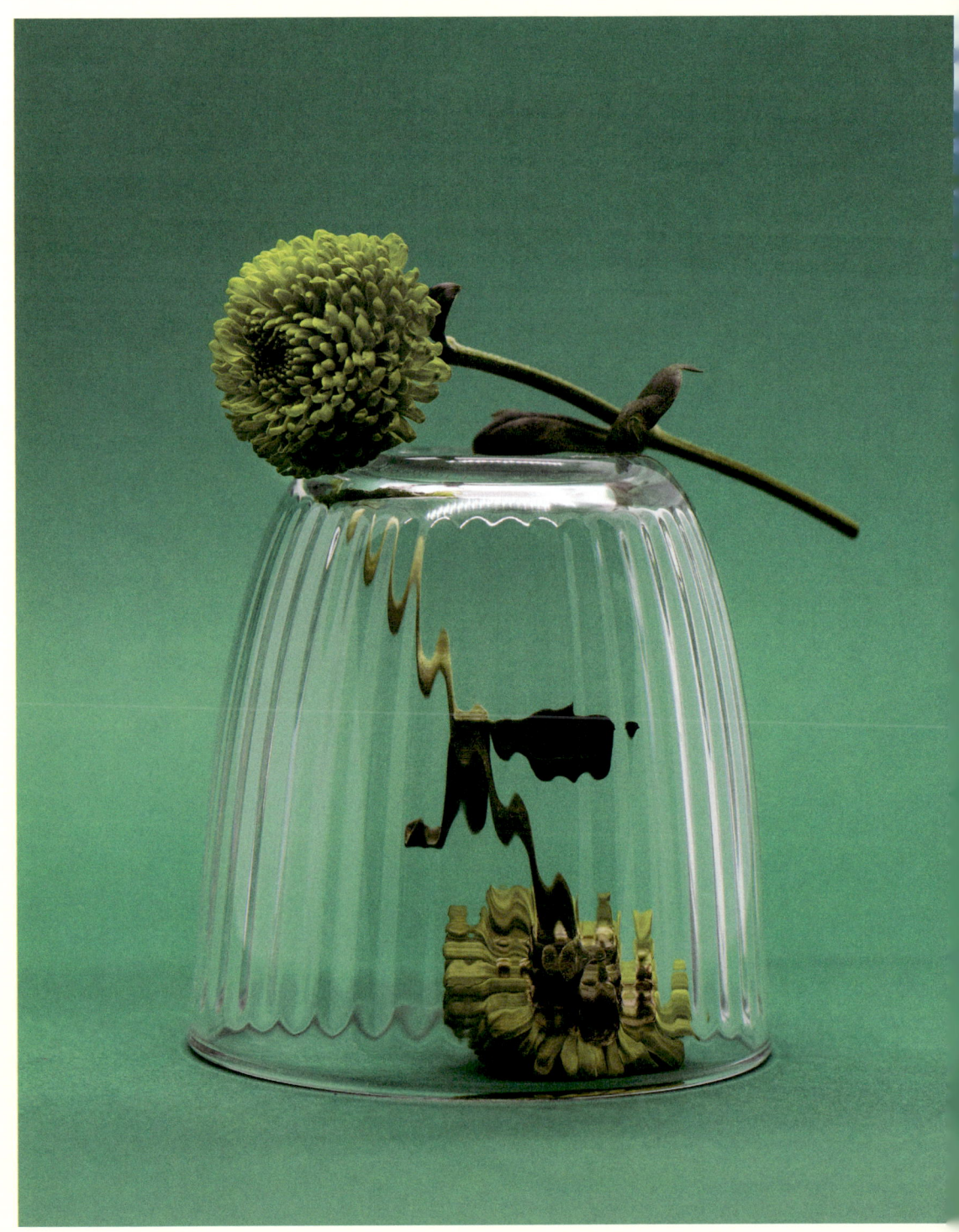

BEEN THERE, MYTHBUSTED THAT

Myth

THE WORLD NEEDS BETTER LEADERSHIP

Truth
THE WORLD ONLY NEEDS SERVANTHOOD

Leadership often emerges as a consequence of effective decision-making. It is the embodiment of the results achieved through thoughtful choices. However, the conventional approach to leadership can lead to egotism and an unending pursuit of self-satisfaction. While I have been recognized as a leader due to the outcomes of my decisions, I've come to realize that true leadership lies in a servanthood mindset. While I initially sought to practice leadership in my early business years, I have found that my effectiveness is amplified when I embrace servanthood instead, with a primary focus on serving my team members.

The prevalent overemphasis on leadership has reached all corners of society, including preteen and young adult circles. Schools and businesses alike seem to prioritize recruiting leaders above all else. This fixation on leadership begs the question: what happens to those who are not deemed leaders? In a team context, not everyone can be the leader. This raises concerns about the well-being of team members who aren't in leadership positions. The pressure to constantly vie for leadership can create unhealthy dynamics within organizations, and the global spread of this "leadership pandemic" demands careful consideration.

It is puzzling when authors claim we can learn leadership skills from Jesus. A deeper examination of the Bible reveals that Jesus consistently emphasized servanthood, never singling out leadership as a crucial life skill. A fellow thinker, Bishop Hwa Yung, penned a compelling book critiquing the veneration of leadership in the church.

When perusing articles and books on leadership, it is worth pondering whether these skills should be exclusive to leaders or whether they apply to any effective team member. Is there truly a unique set of attributes reserved for leaders? This prompts us to reconsider the essence of leadership itself. Ultimately, I do not find it necessary to invent elaborate terms like "level five leaders," "upside down leaders," or "unleaders" to illustrate my point. The concept of servanthood encapsulates the heart of the matter.

Servanthood offers a consistent approach that aligns with the practice of "loving thy neighbor as thyself." It transcends titles and positions, allowing everyone to contribute effectively within a group setting. This approach emphasizes collaboration, empathy, and mutual respect—all of which are crucial for the growth and harmony of any organization.

Let's challenge the prevailing mindset of leadership worship and consider the profound impact that embracing servanthood can have on our lives and the world around us. The pursuit of excellence need not be confined to a leadership framework; it can flourish within the context of servanthood, fostering an environment of unity, compassion, and shared success.

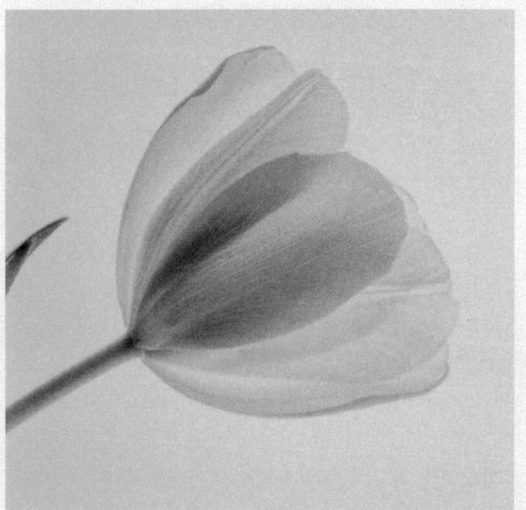

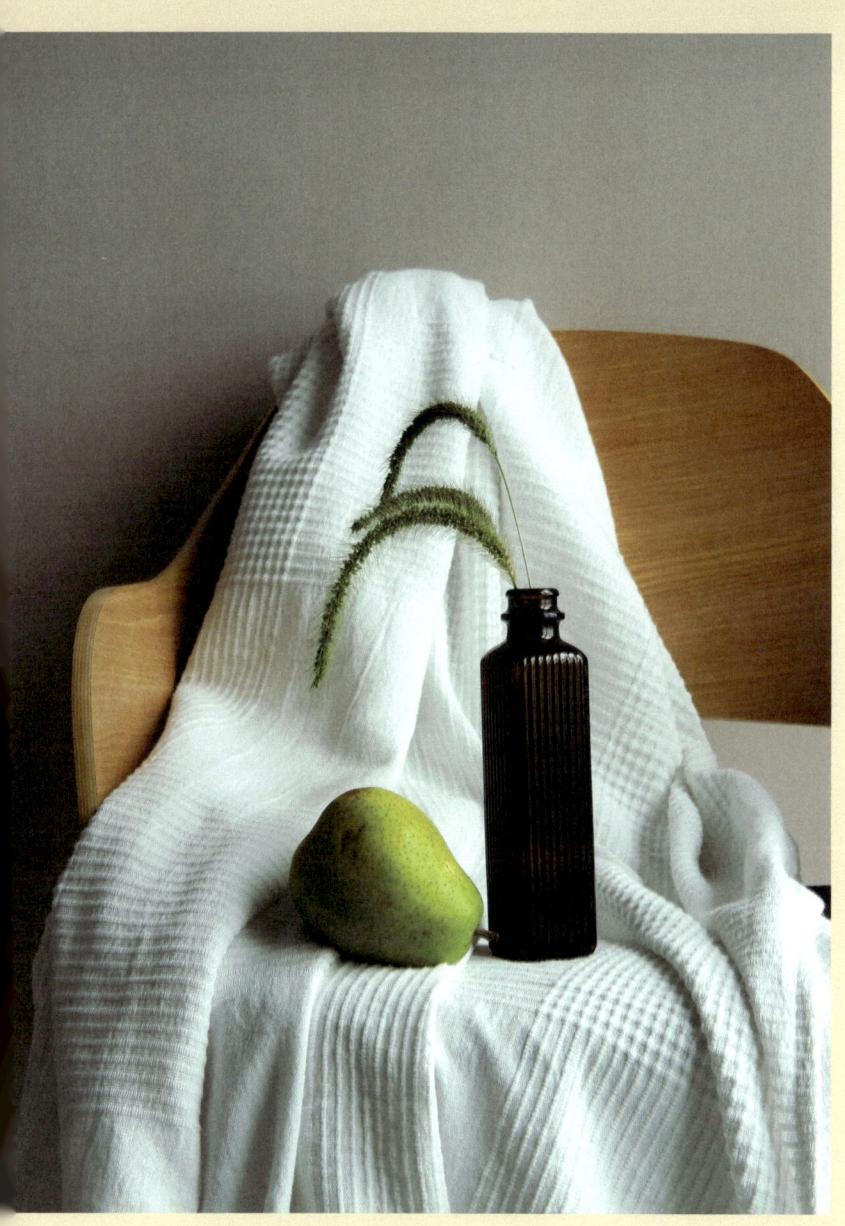

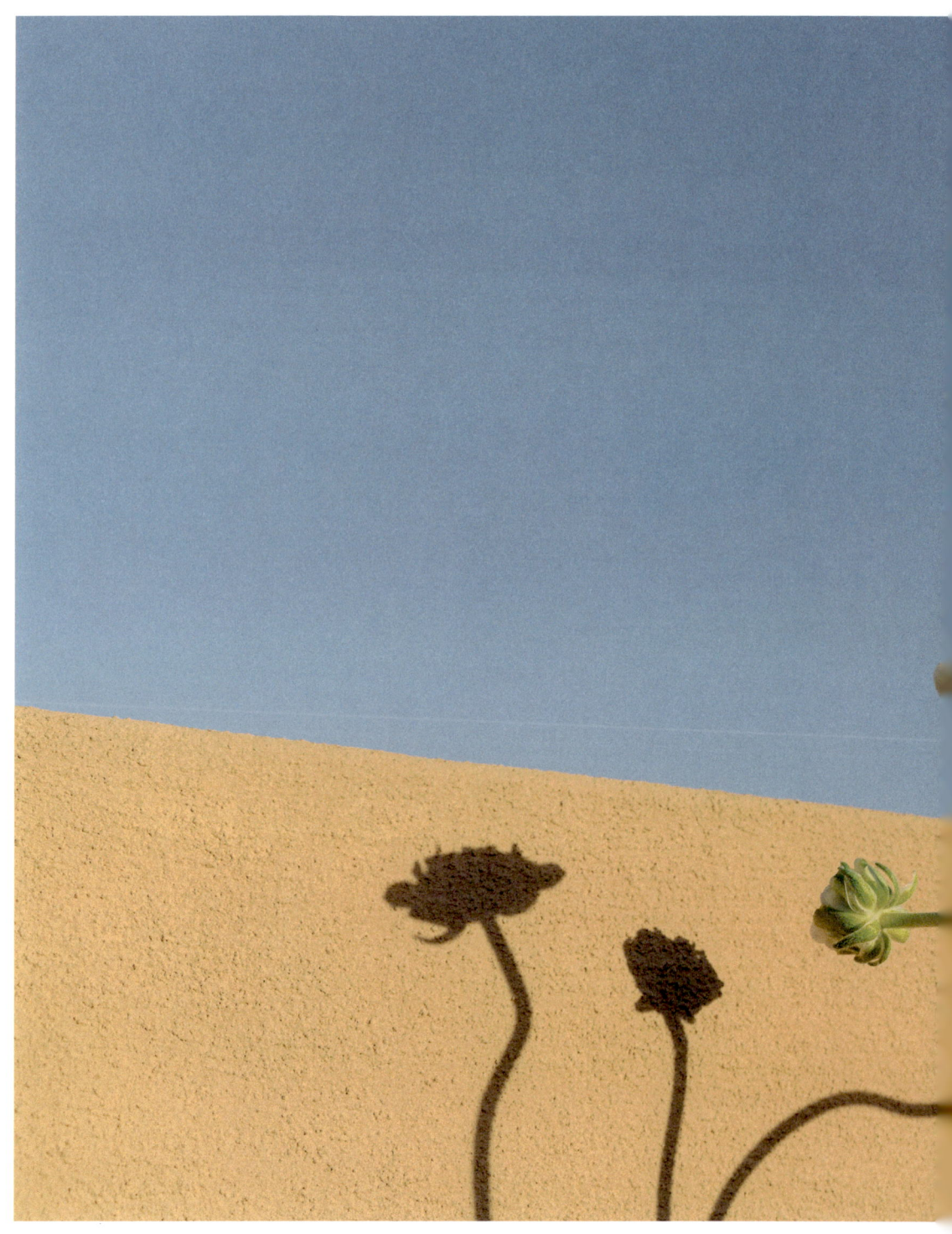

BEEN THERE, MYTHBUSTED THAT

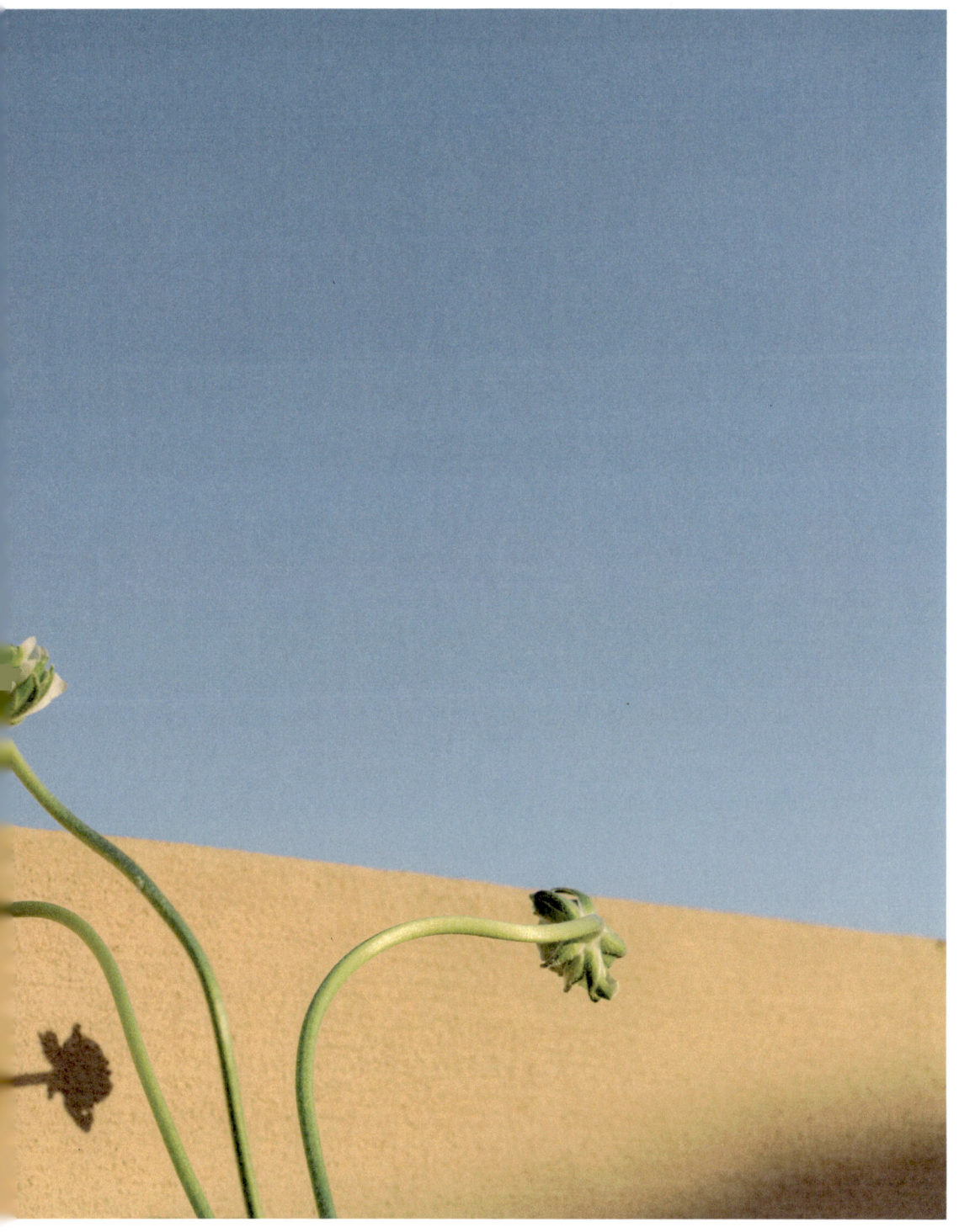

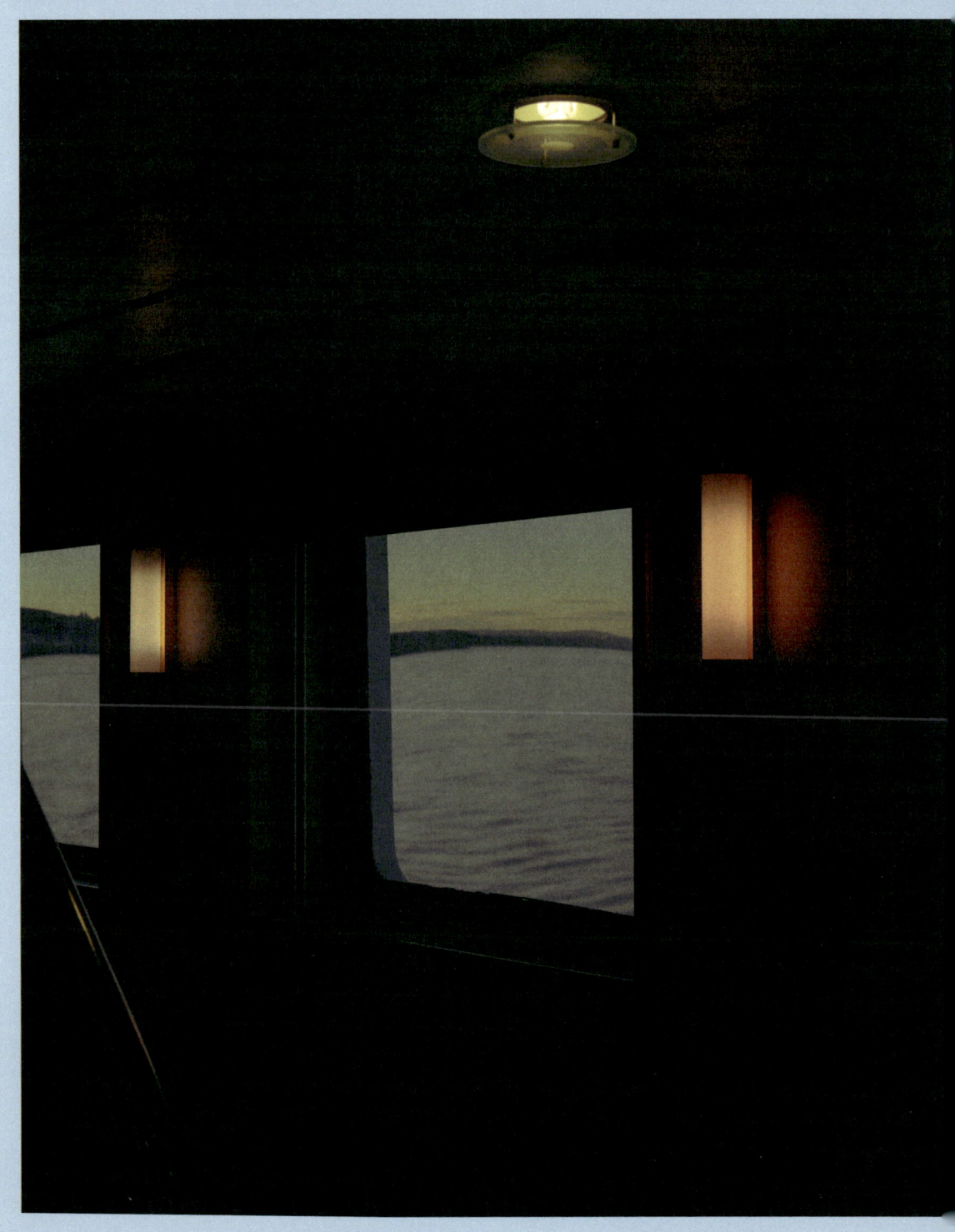

BEEN THERE, MYTHBUSTED THAT

Myth

CULTURE REPLACES
LEADERSHIP TRAINING

Truth

CULTURE IS A RESULT OF EXCELLENT RECRUITMENT

Following the excessive pursuit and promotion of leadership, the tide is turning with more and more examples of failed leadership everywhere. Now, instead of injecting great "leadership" into organizations, we have new consultants and programs trying to inject great "culture." Organizations falsely believe this will somehow improve a company's performance and health, but it is just another false prognosis.

From my forty-three years of business experience, I can loudly proclaim that "culture" is not a program. It is not something one can buy and implement. Culture is the amalgamation and expression of every team member's unique personality and gifts being brought into the business. It is why employee recruitment is such a top priority for every company; whoever works in the company will play a role in defining the culture of the company. Culture, therefore, is not something we shape from the outside. It is a process we nurture from within by assembling a team of employees that share the same values, beliefs, and morals. It is a continual process once we realize that the culture of a company changes each time an employee joins or exits the team. Monitoring if a company's culture remains healthy is one of the most difficult and essential tasks of a CEO.

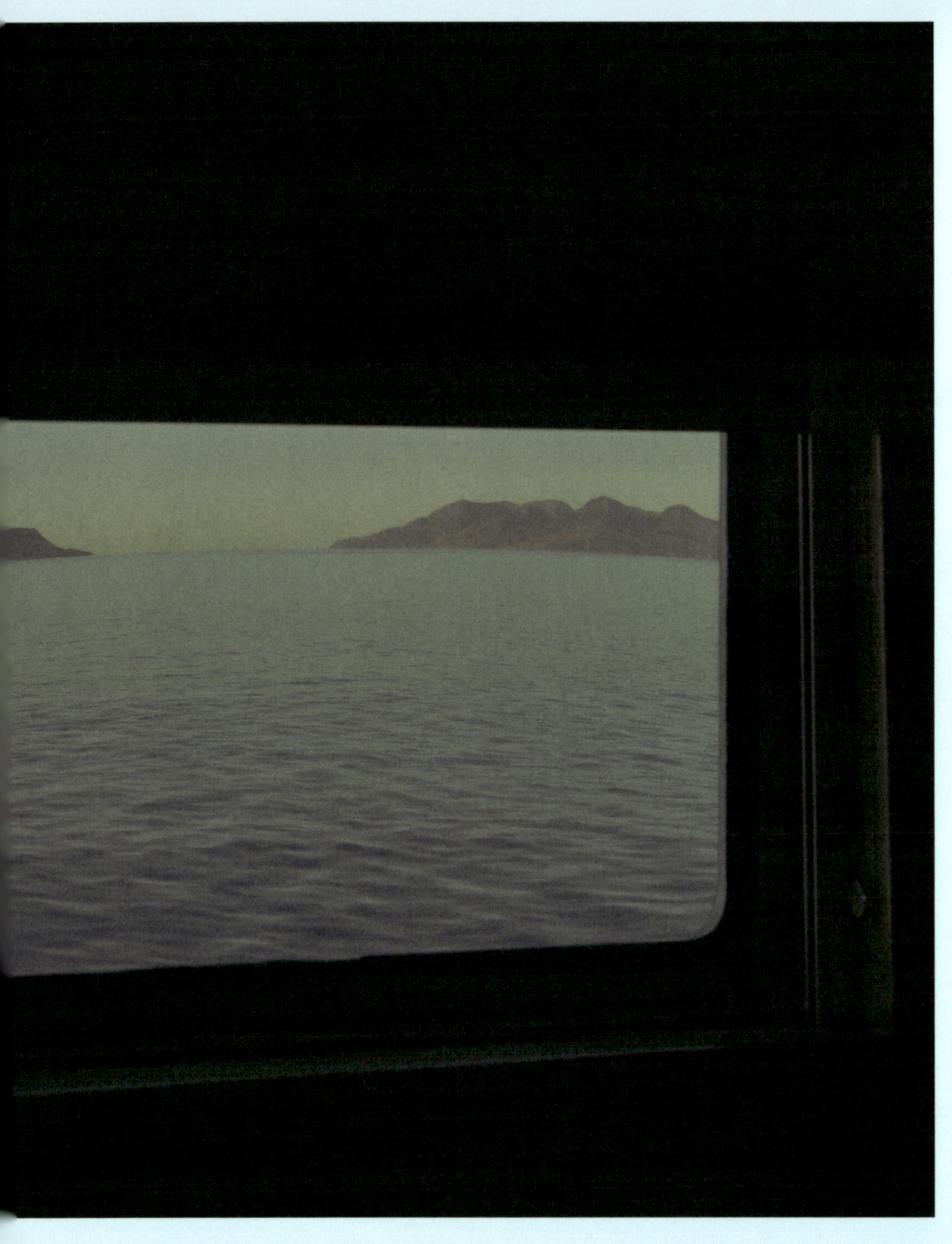

BEEN THERE, MYTHBUSTED THAT

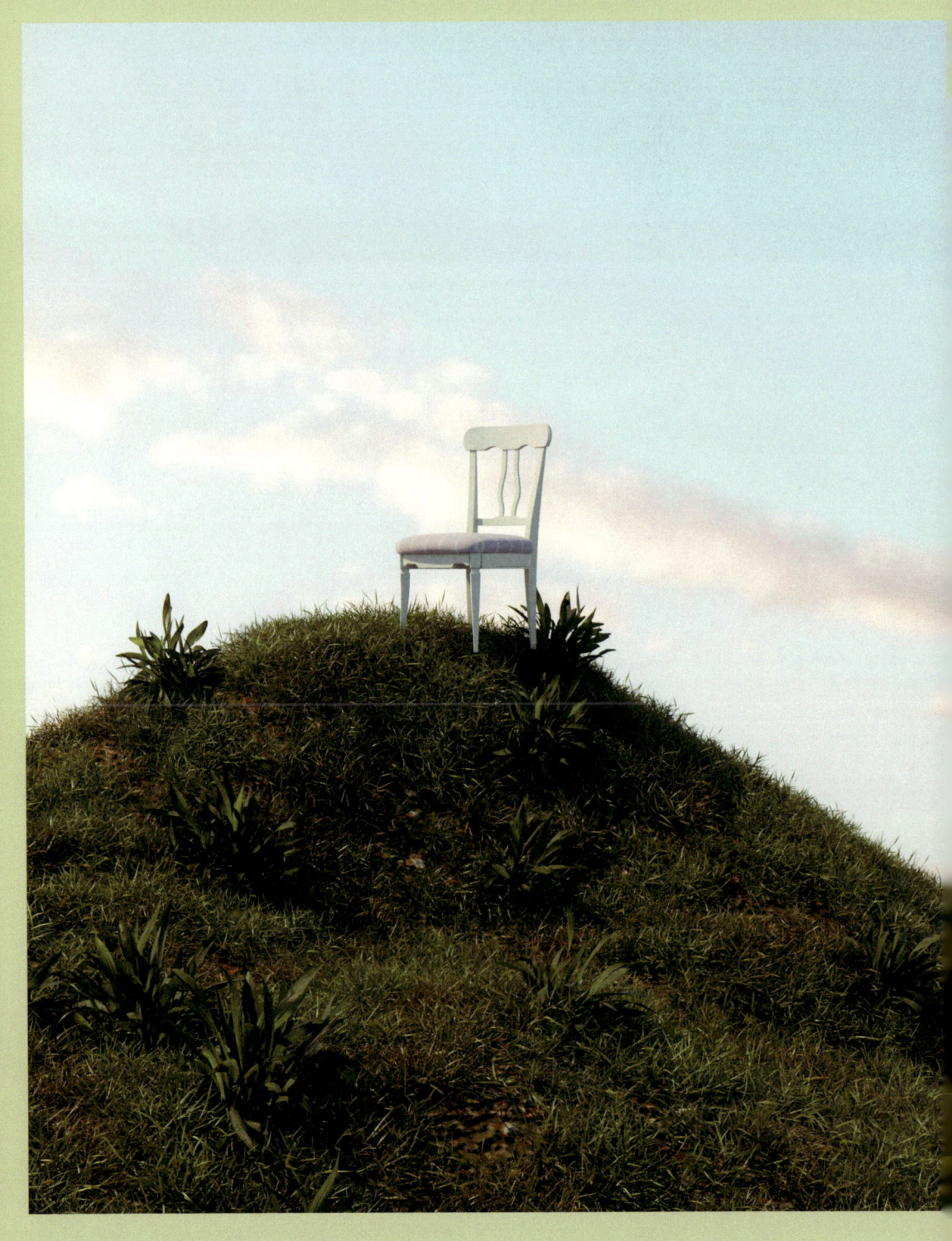

BEEN THERE, MYTHBUSTED THAT

Myth
I AM A PERFECTIONIST

Truth

I STRIVE TO BE MORE EXCELLENT DAILY

Some people declare themselves to be "perfectionists" as a way to express their struggle with identity. For myself and my companies, being perfect is not and has never been the goal. Rather, being excellent—through continuous learning and daily improvement—is our practice.

Being perfect is a dead-end proposal. What does one do after achieving perfection?

Instead, I follow my father's practice: aiming to be more excellent today than I was yesterday and striving to be even more excellent tomorrow.. Being excellent is based on a relative mindset; it is not a competitive statement against another person. It is a personal challenge every day and, in my experience, joy and satisfaction stem from the positive process of learning and self-improvement.

So, as I repeat at my companies' quarterly meetings: unlike organizations where management or shareholders demand perfection and severely penalize mistakes, we do *not* expect or aim for perfection. In fact, when a company is growing at a healthy pace, having problems is a reality to be accepted and an opportunity for embracing improvement. A healthily growing company should be constantly trying new processes, introducing fresh products, and encountering challenges from competition. To expect everything to run perfectly is pure fantasy and sheer arrogance. Also, without problems, why would we need employees? There is a special enjoyment found in solving problems together, working together, and growing together—imperfectly but beautifully.

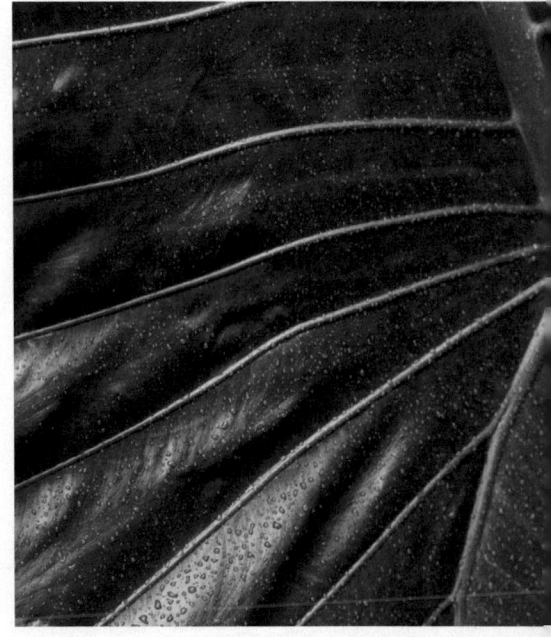

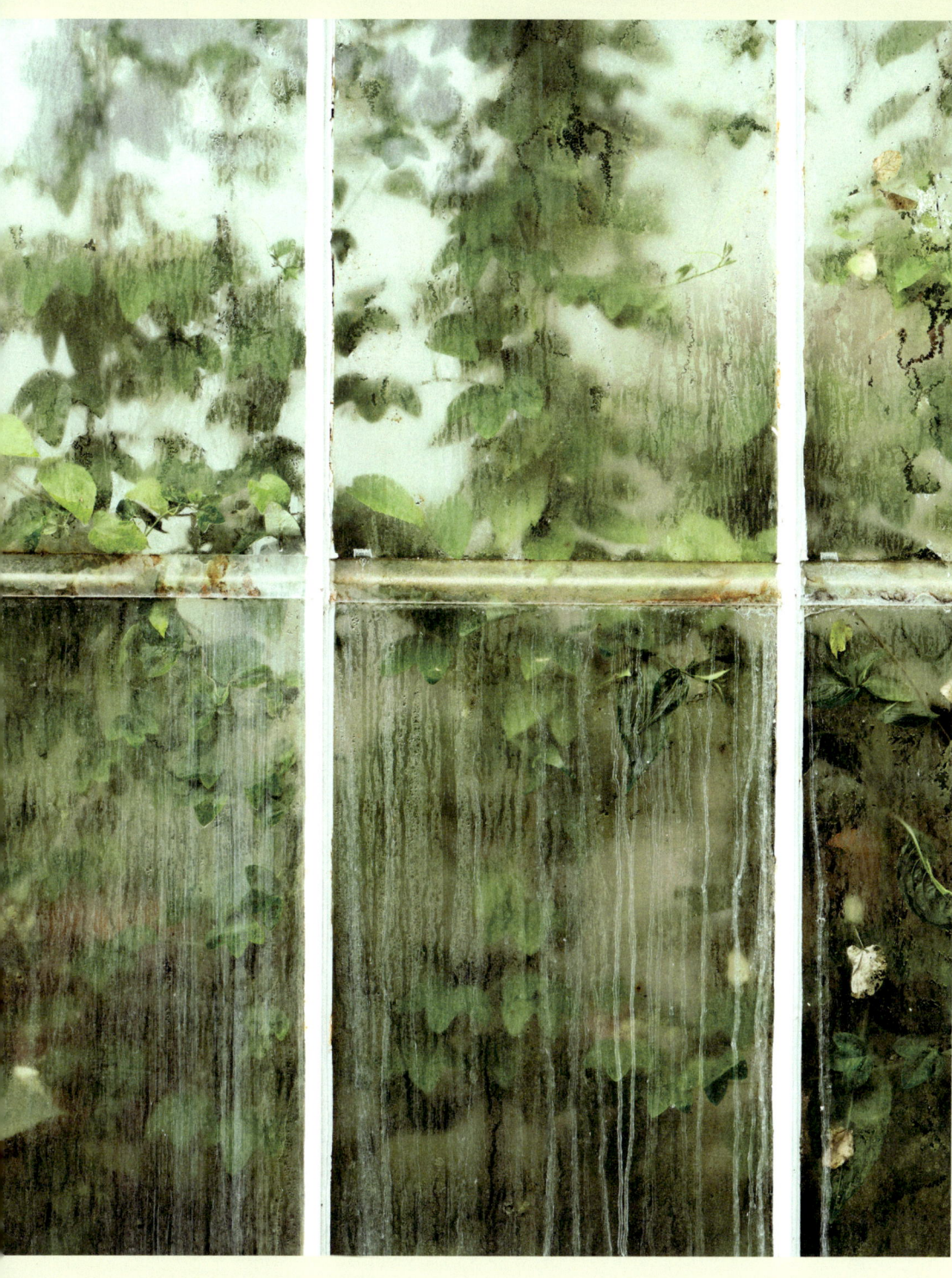

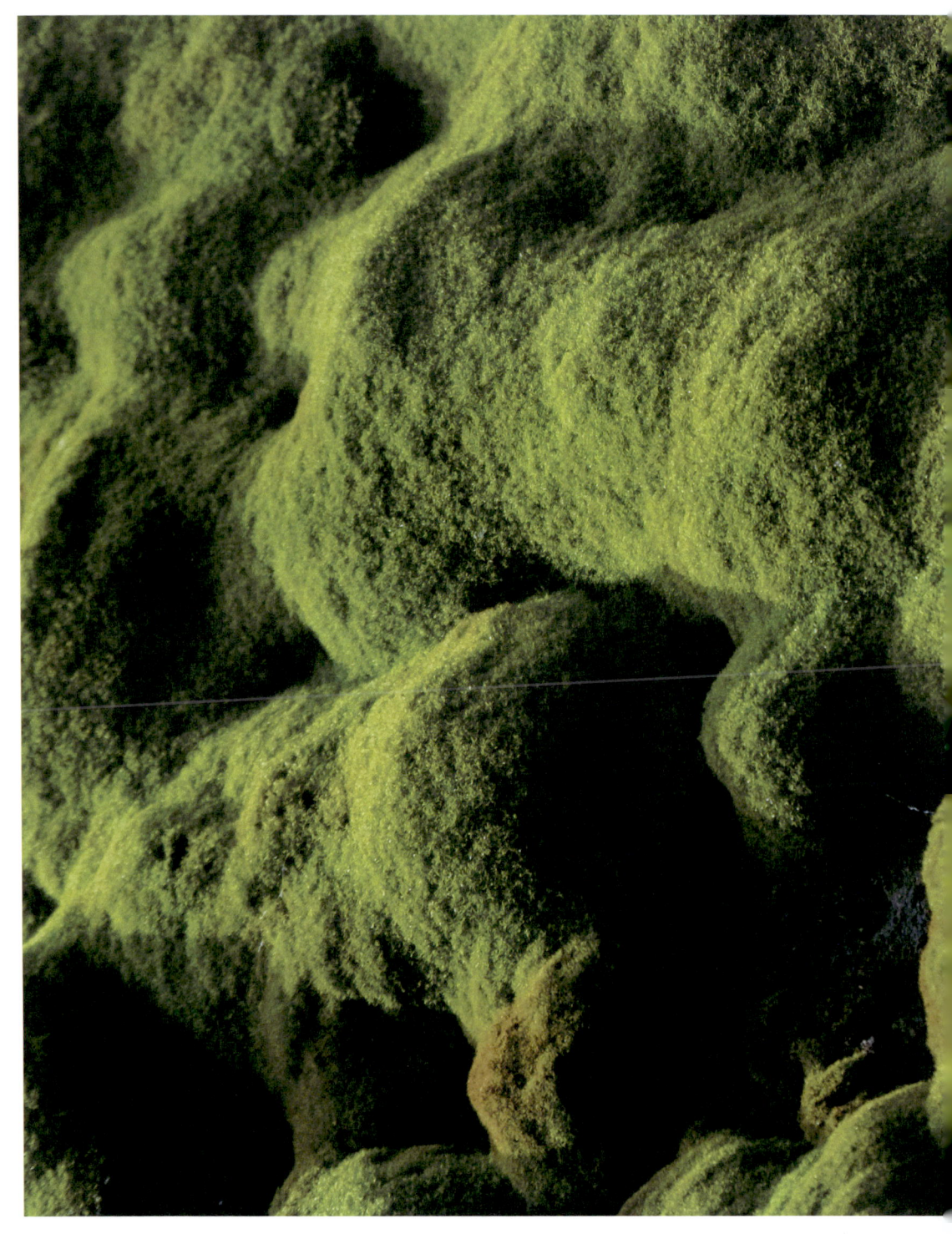

BEEN THERE, MYTHBUSTED THAT

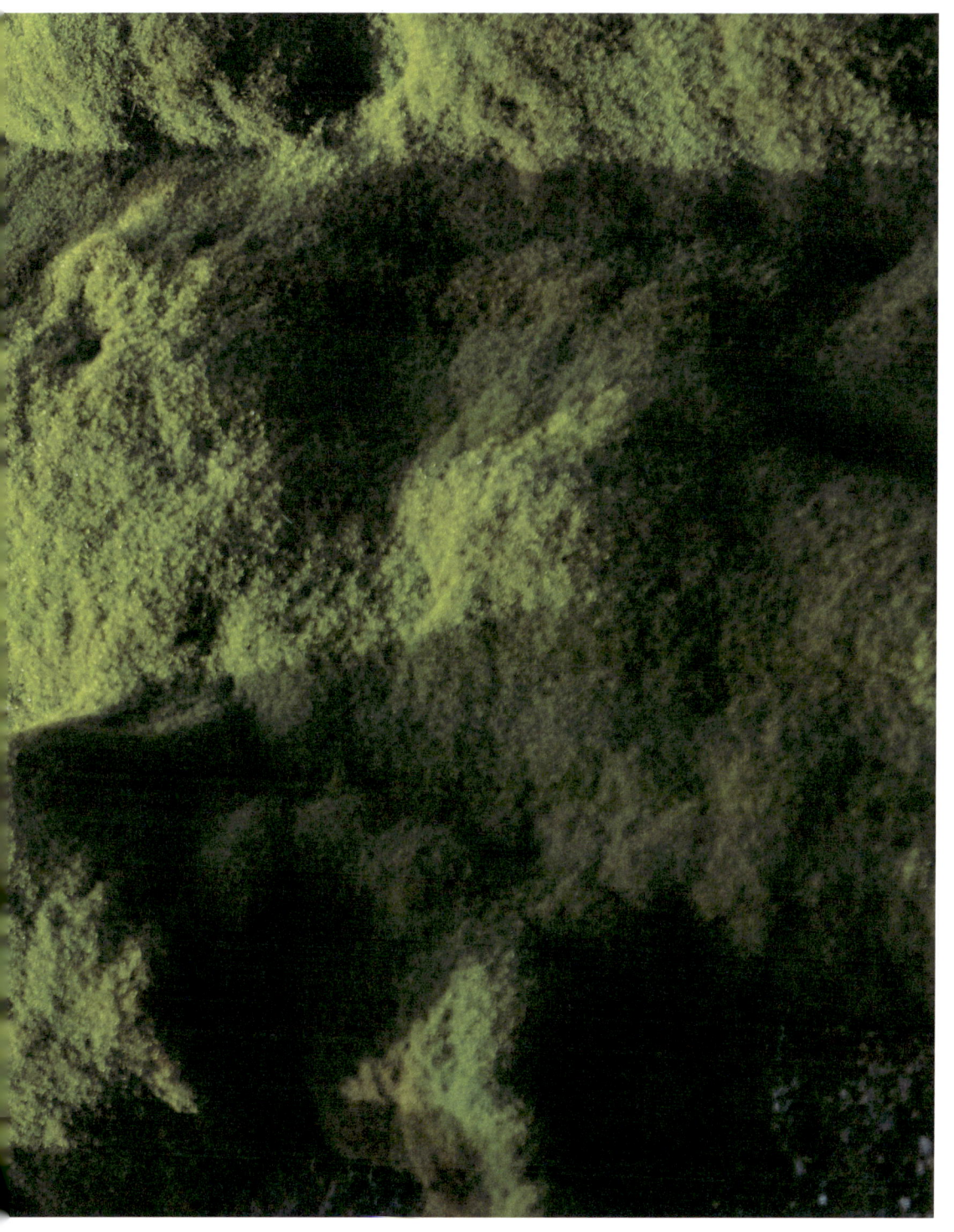

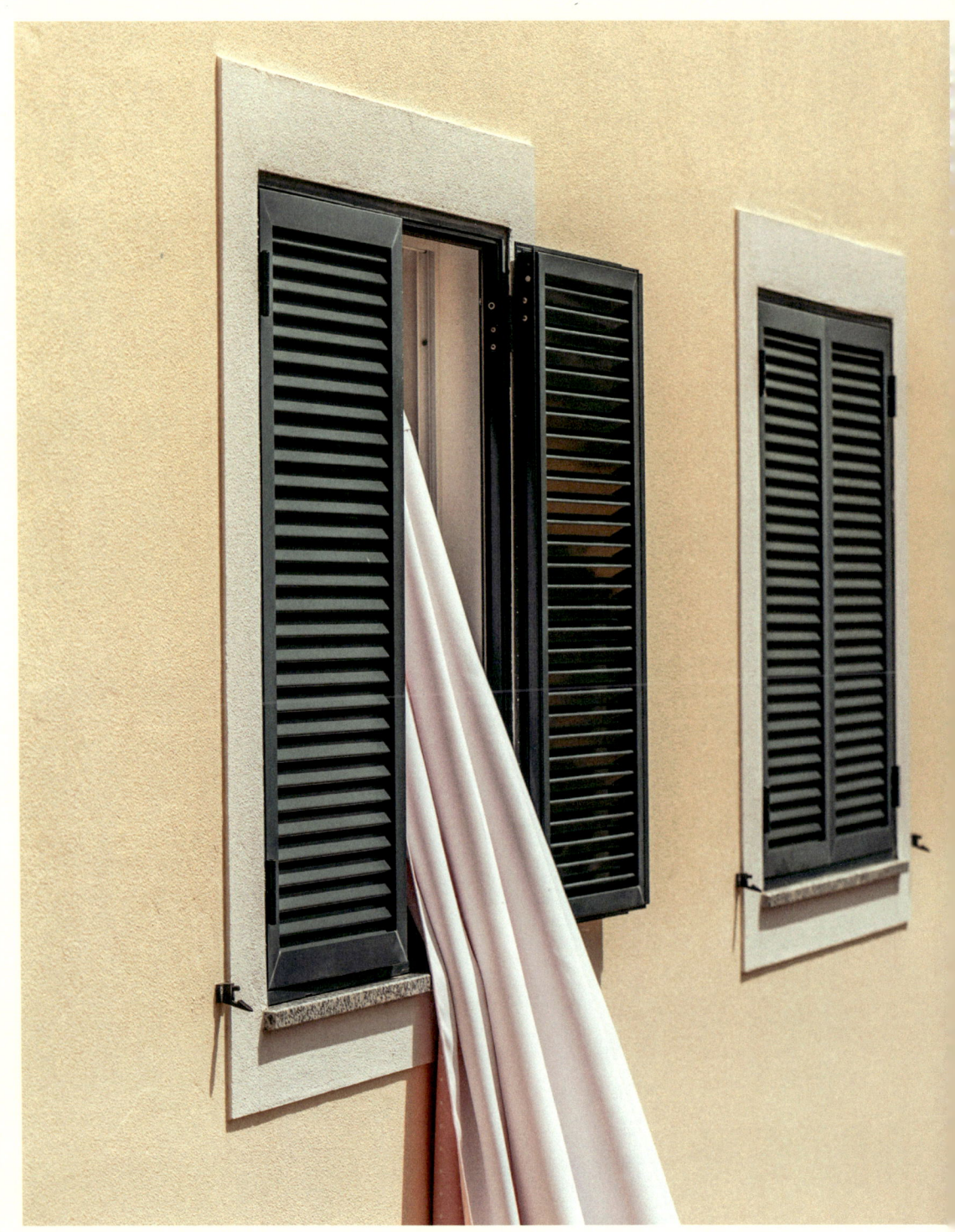

BEEN THERE, MYTHBUSTED THAT

Myth

WE ARE
WHAT WE DO

Truth

WE DO BECAUSE WE ARE

Being vs doing

We are taught to reinforce our sense of identity through accomplishments at a very young age. My parents were proud because I was always one of the top three students on school tests. To be competitive and to win seemed like the only goal in life. I skipped fourth grade, graduated valedictorian from high school, and entered Harvard University as a sophomore (skipping my freshman year).

When I started my own business in 1990, becoming the wealthiest person was the goal; it was the only way I knew how to derive any form of identity. Therefore, I did a lot of doing—enrolling in leadership training classes and working long hours with no end in sight. While I did gain some success, this goal ultimately limited me when it came to experiencing a truly peaceful and joyful life.

Once I transferred CEO responsibilities to my son, I began to seriously contemplate what I should do next. I no longer had daily responsibilities, and, while I still advised my son, I encountered a great amount of free time I had no idea how to fill.

Coincidentally, 2016 was a challenging year for me, theologically and philosophically, because of the widening discourse in politics and culture all over the globe. My continuing dissatisfaction with organized religion prompted me to seek higher learning at the Fuller Theological Seminary, and it was there I began to explore focusing on *being* rather than *doing*.

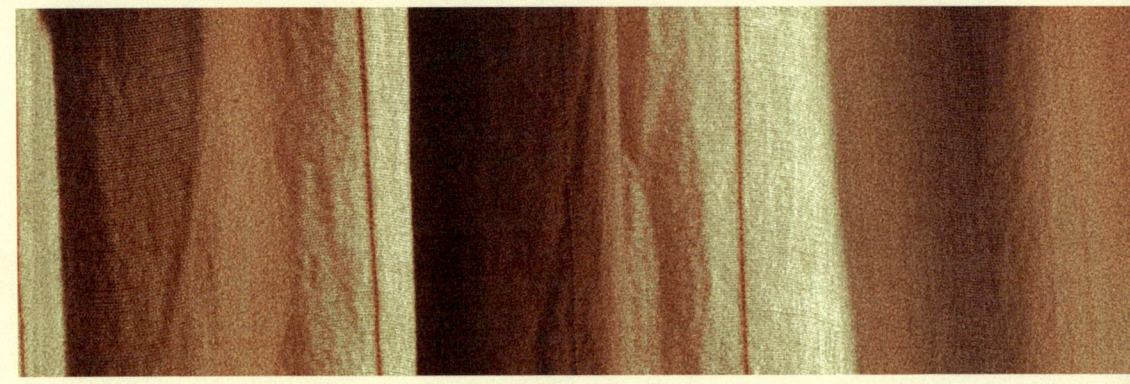

Focusing on being is all about how we can be more like Christ and allow Christ to take full control of our lives. When we start with Christ's being, our doing will automatically be Christlike. Instead of focusing on our doing, our priority in life is to focus on our being. From a non-religious angle, this is our character, morals, and ethics. For me, instead of inventing my own character subjectively, I found using Jesus Christ as a model to be much simpler and freer.

That is my current practice and, even though I do not focus on my doing, my schedule is full of "divine appointments." Divine appointments refer to my willingness to pay attention to random occurrences with people throughout the day, which naturally lead to more random encounters and projects. Instead of focusing on the outcomes of these random projects, I focus on my motivation to engage: to be obedient and patient, without trying to build up my own personal reputation or earn more money. By living life in this

way, and focusing on being, I see each random occurrence as glorious, fun, and creative—unburdened by a need to *do* things a certain way or achieve a specific result.

All of this said, some form of "doing" can be good. Having aspirations, hopes, and dreams are not inherently evil things—and you need to take action to achieve them. However, my main caution is to stay away from "doings" that are fueled by selfish motivations to accumulate wealth, success, accolades, and earthly possessions. That is why the primary focus is to work on our being; in building our character and faith, we get to know the character and will of Christ and die to self. Our identity is then based on who we are instead of what we do or possess, and the correct kinds of "doing" become more natural.

1. Working on our being

- This aspect emphasizes personal growth, character development, and spiritual transformation. It involves cultivating virtues such as love, kindness, integrity, humility, and compassion—reflecting God's nature.
- Engaging in self-reflection, prayer, and study of Scripture can help individuals deepen their understanding of God's will and align their lives with His teachings.
- Developing a Christlike work ethic, where honesty, diligence, and a humble attitude are evident in one's labor, is part of working on oneself to become more like God.
- Prioritizing relationships and serving others within the workplace fosters an environment of grace and love.

2. Working On Doing That Comes From Correctly Being

- This aspect acknowledges that work can lead to personal achievement, financial prosperity, and the establishment of a good reputation.
- Seeking excellence in one's profession and pursuing career advancement are legitimate aspirations, provided they do not conflict with ethical principles or neglect the well-being of others.
- Building a reputable name in the workplace can create opportunities to influence others positively and serve as a platform for sharing one's faith and values.
- Gaining wealth through ethical means enables individuals to be more generous in supporting noble causes and helping those in need

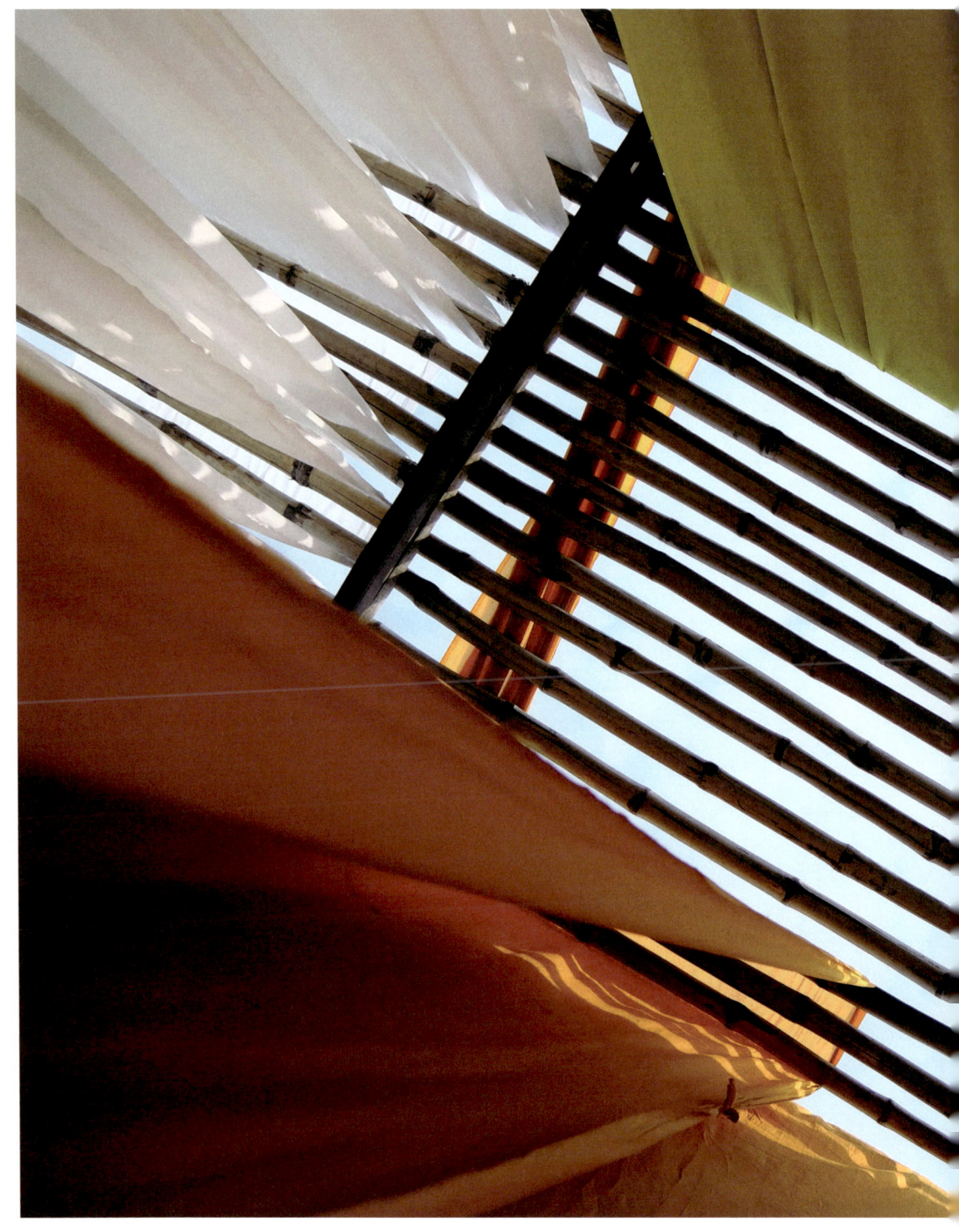

BEEN THERE, MYTHBUSTED THAT

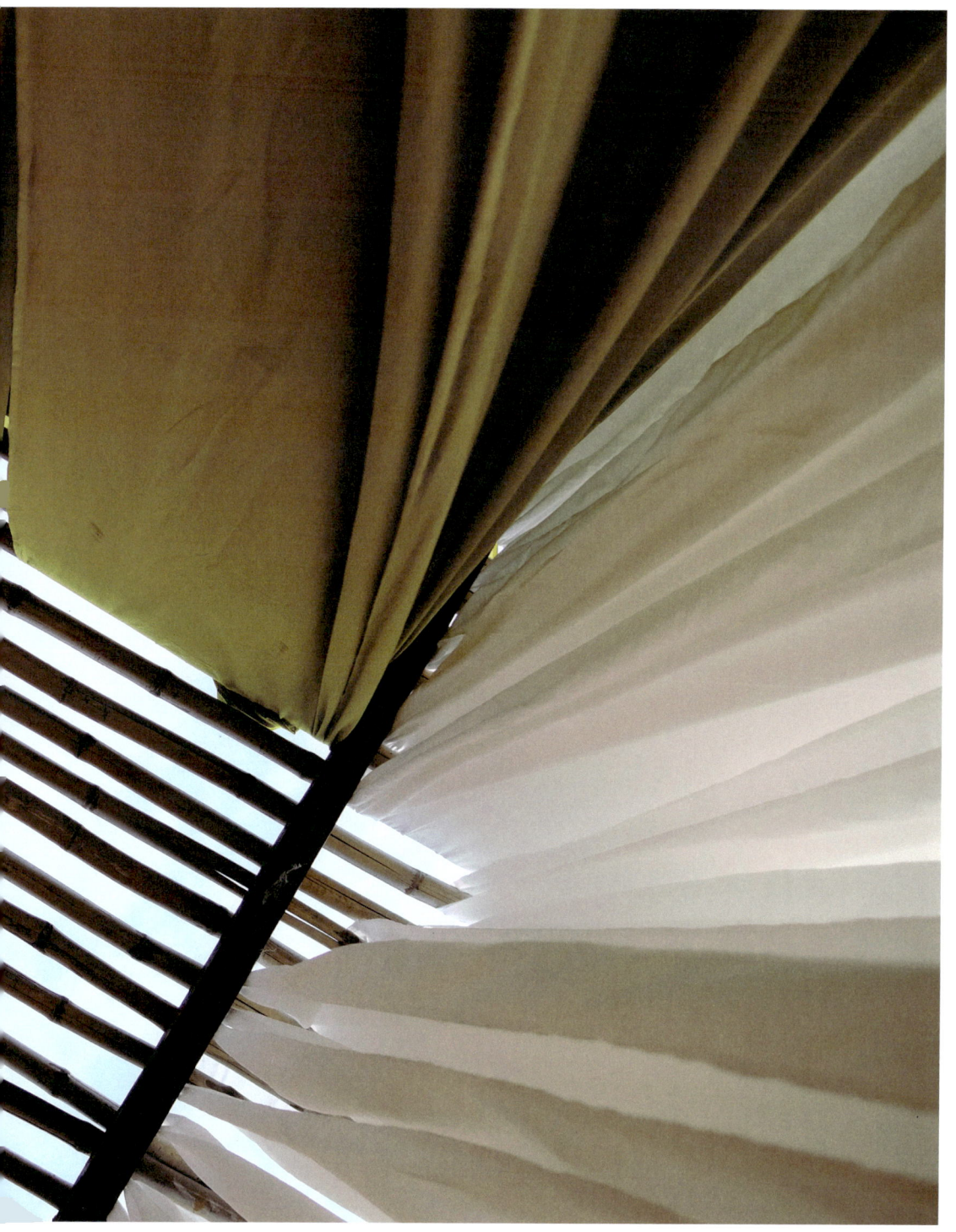

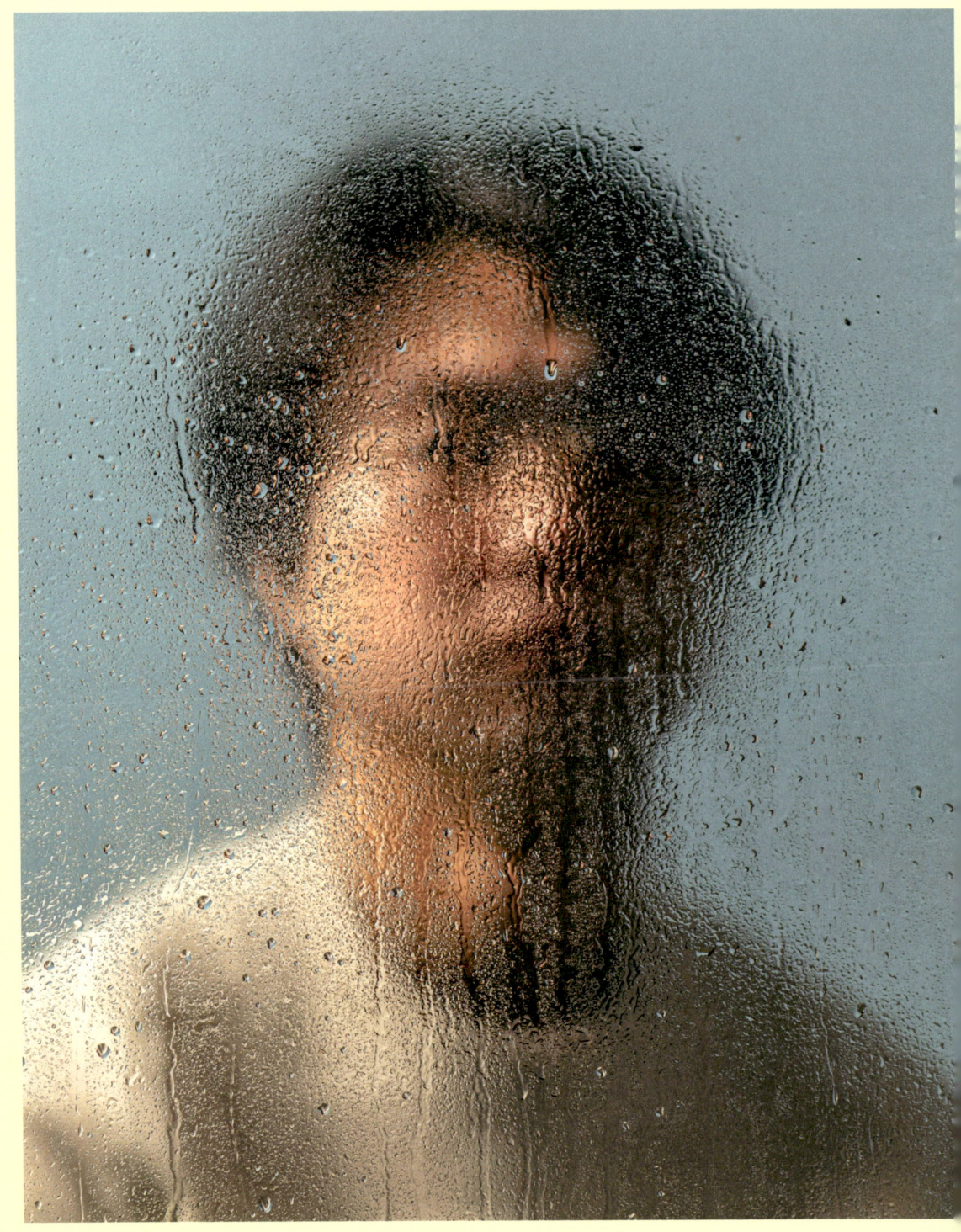

BEEN THERE, MYTHBUSTED THAT

Myth
WE NEED TO FIND OUR TRUE SELVES

Truth
FUSE OUR IDENTITY WITH JESUS CHRIST

Identity crisis

There is an identity crisis sweeping the world, introducing confusion and despair among young people. They struggle to find their identity, thinking they can primarily define it by what they *do* or what they *have*: their accomplishments, accolades, reputations, and possessions. When so much identity becomes formed by shallow external forces and objects, there is nothing grounding the person in the painful realities of life. It is detrimental for the individual and society, leading to culture wars—a communal confusion about what is ultimately good versus evil, and true versus fake.

This issue is true for Christians too. Addressing the polarization of Christianity in America, I wrote the following essay in my founder's update for my nonprofit's website:

When we do not fully identify with the character of Jesus Christ, we default to doing things *for* God as a way to be good and faithful followers. We assume that our work and effort will replace the need for our crucifixion. Based upon my observations, Christians have replaced the dead weight of sin and death with the dead weight of good works in the name of God and for God. The popular, but erroneous, attention to "my calling," "my vocation," and "my ministry" are reflections of an identity confusion about who we are and what we should do. Why? Because we have been taught by tradition and societal pressures that our identity is based upon our doing, which aids the accumulation of possessions, accomplishments, accolades, and, ultimately, anticipated rewards from God.

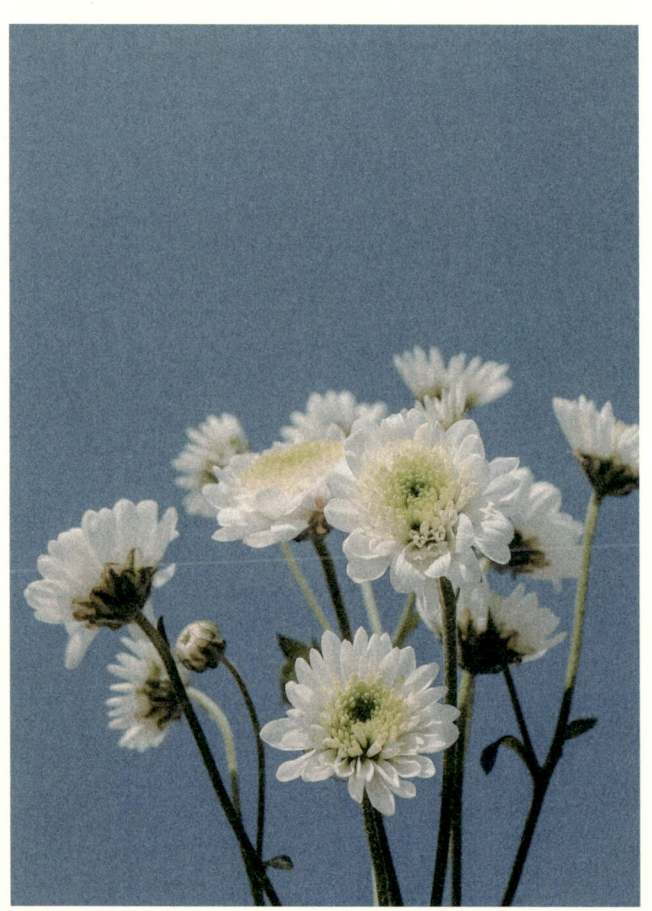

BEEN THERE, MYTHBUSTED THAT

I have come to the understanding that my identity comes from the crucifixion of old self-centered identities. I allow my doing to be a natural outflow of the Holy Spirit when the identity of Jesus Christ replaces my old one.

Christians have replaced the dead weight of sin and death with the dead weight of good works. Instead of being free, believers are anxious, worried, angry, dissatisfied, and frustrated. Throughout church history, they have thought that the world is heading in the wrong direction and that Christians need to "do something" to save the world. Why? So that the new heaven, new earth, and the new Jerusalem will come? And that, only through our diligent and faithful work, God will fulfill His promise? Is that really what the Bible teaches us? Is that really God's will?

To me, the law of sin and death is like gravity. It is a law no one can defy. However, when we get into a hot air balloon and rise (thanks to the law of thermodynamics), we can defy gravity. In a similar fashion, the law of the spirit of life can alleviate the dead weight, lifting us up. We need to climb into the hot air balloon of Christ. When we rely on our own work and effort in the form of our calling, vocation, or ministry, we remain on the ground, unable to escape the gravity of sin and death. We add unnecessary stress and burden ourselves, thinking striving for "good works" can save us, but it is not the law of good works that will set us free. It is the law of the spirit of life.

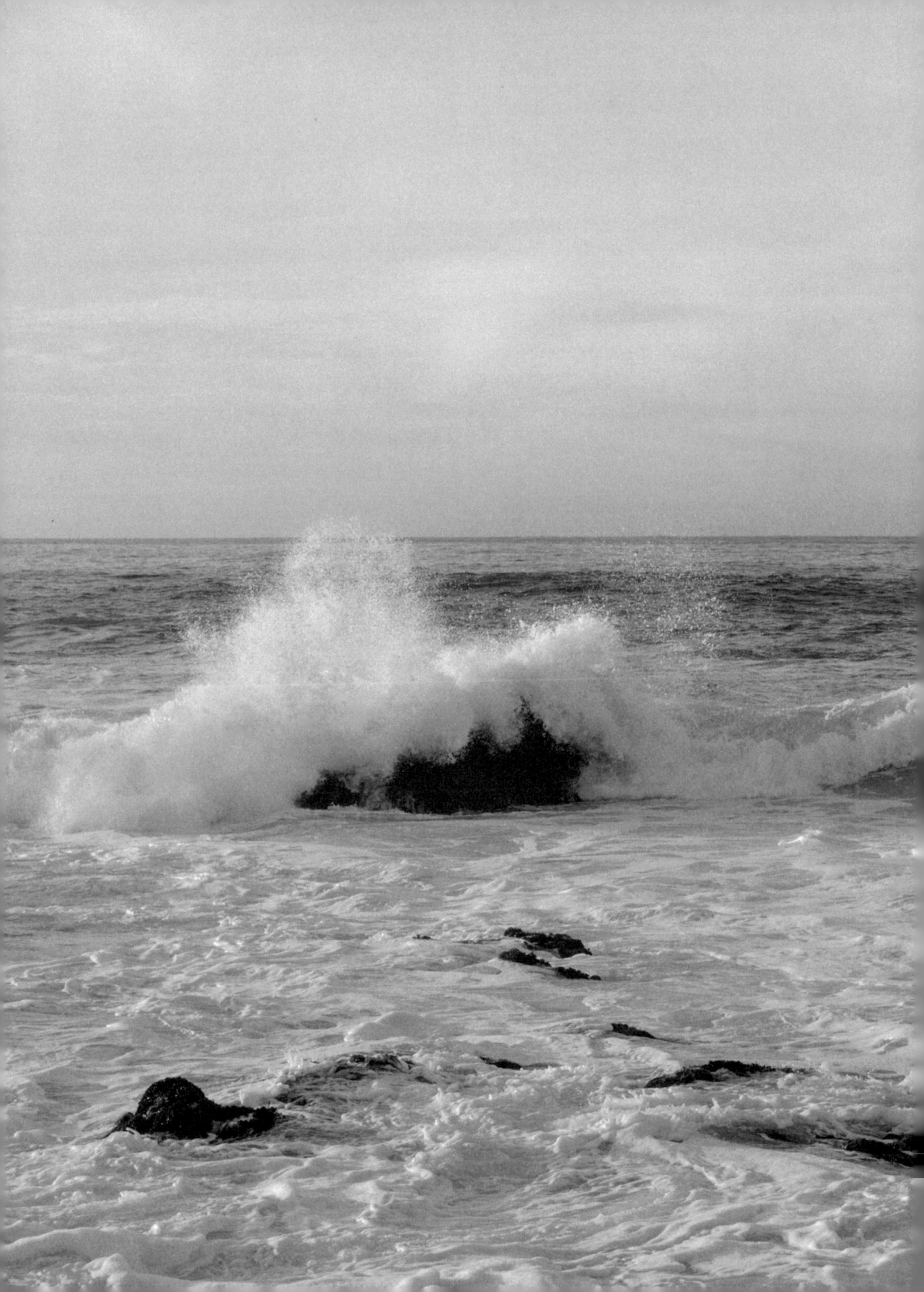